PRAISE FOR THIS BOOK

"Accessible and informative, this agile volume on African Catholicism after the Second Vatican Council questions much of the received wisdom about the alleged 'success' of the Catholic Church in Africa in the last few decades. Bringing together five articles by George Neumayr on Catholicism in Ivory Coast and a few more essays by other authors addressing the broader issues of inculturation and liturgical reform, this collection will introduce the reader to an ecclesial reality far more problematic and fractured than the naively optimistic portrayals often found in Catholic publications. In particular, Kwasniewski's and Salvucci's reflections on the demise of the traditional Mass and the impact of the Zaire rite on African Catholicism offer an important critique of the simplistic accounts of liturgical inculturation promoted by Catholic media."

—**THOMAS CATTOI**, PhD; William and Barbara Moran Chair in Early Christian Theology and Interreligious Relations, Pontifical University of Saint Thomas Aquinas (Angelicum), Rome

"Post-Vatican II scholarship on the Catholic Church in Africa privileges a quasi-dogmatised narrative of a continental pastoral triumph premised on inculturation, and realised in all-around growth: multitudes of Catholics, crowded churches, exuberant liturgies, seminaries bursting at the seams with hopefuls for the priestly ministry. Dr. Kwasniewski's book dares to challenge this narrative by questioning its assumptions. Though exploratory in scope and approach, the book exposes the fundamental ideological fiction that arbitrarily sets

Vatican II as 'ground zero' from which the authentic growth and development of the Church in Africa are alleged to derive. While the dominant narrative renders invisible the manifold fruits of heroic missionary endeavours that established the faith on the African continent and drew forth the witness of martyrdom, this book serves a rehabilitative function. The book serves as a welcome, though tentative, corrective foray into a fraudulent historiography of the Catholic Church in Africa based on eurocentric ideological preoccupations of difference and the other, the exoticization of perceptions of cultural particularity, and, above all, the ahistorical rupture with pre-Vatican II foundations of the Church in Africa harking back to the patristic period. Dr. Kwasniewski's book unsettles ideological certainties in the service of Christ and His Church."

—**MICHAEL KAKOOZA**, PhD, Strategic Management, Eastern Africa

"The entirety of this book, brimming with intelligent observations and illustrated with unknown and appealing historical examples, will trigger conversations that should not be postponed any more. I hope that it will promote a sublime liturgy and the restoration of the epic missionary spirit that seeks the conversion of all to the Catholic Religion, not only in Africa but to the ends of the earth."

—**FR. FEDERICO HIGHTON**, PhD, ThD; co-founder of two sub-Saharan parishes; Omnes Gentes Project Director

"Recently I spent some time in Uganda, a profoundly religious country, nearly 90% of whose citizens are Christian. Among the reasons I went was to see if the hope many Americans have that Africa might 'save the Church' has much warrant. This book reflects what I saw: if Africa is to play this role, it must resist the bad influence of the West. My impression of Ugandan people is that they have a deep and genuine faith, a natural modesty, ready generosity, refreshing transparency, and a joyful reverence. They love their Jesus. I went to one traditional Latin Mass and several Novus Ordo Masses, marked by a clear awareness of the presence of the sacred. I believe the TLM would be, in certain ways, less 'foreign' to the faith, history, and liturgical sensibilities of Africans than is the Novus Ordo. This book is an excellent introduction to the beautiful faith of Africans and the compatibility of the TLM with that faith."

—**JANET E. SMITH**, PhD, moral theologian and advocate for Ugandan seminarians

IS AFRICAN CATHOLICISM
A "VATICAN II SUCCESS STORY"?

In Memoriam
GEORGE NEUMAYR
July 16, 1972–January 19, 2023

Is African Catholicism a "Vatican II Success Story"?

Questioning the
Conventional Narrative

GEORGE NEUMAYR
❖
CLAUDIO SALVUCCI
❖
PETER KWASNIEWSKI
❖
AN AFRICAN SEMINARIAN

Os Justi Press

Os Justi Press
P.O. Box 21814
Lincoln, NE 68542
www.osjustipress.com

Send inquiries to
info@osjustipress.com

ISBN 978-1-965303-07-8 (paperback)
ISBN 978-1-965303-08-5 (hardcover)
ISBN 978-1-965303-09-2 (ebook)

Layout by Michael Schrauzer
Cover by Julian Kwasniewski
Cover image:
"Un feu de branchages à Yamoussoukro vers 1992,"
photo by Rc1959, CC by 4.0, cropped.

CONTENTS

PREFACE

GEORGE NEUMAYR, WHO WAS AN acquaintance of mine, had wanted to write a book about Catholicism in Africa. His untimely death, the suddenness of which shocked everyone, prevented him from ever completing that project. However, he had made a not insignificant start on it with his five articles for *The American Spectator* on the situation in Ivory Coast. When I read them, it struck me that this could be the kernel of a book that might, to some extent, fill the need for a treatment of this subject, if augmented with relevant essays and articles by other authors.

The need for it is glaring, because the conventional view is that "Catholicism is booming in Africa"—indeed, that Africa should be seen as the one continent where the Second Vatican Council has yielded indisputable good fruits. We will see indications that this, sadly, is not the case. Many surprises are in store for the trustful adherent of the New Springtime narrative who reads the following pages. Even if this brief study cannot substitute for a yet-to-be-written thorough examination of all the statistics of growth and decline, and their relationship with preconciliar and postconciliar modes of Catholicism, it nevertheless suggests that, at very least, we ought to exercise greater caution in utilizing Africa as a success story for reformed Catholicism.

I would like to express my thanks to Lucia "Lucy" VanBerkum of *The American Spectator* for granting permission to republish George's articles as chapters 1 through 5 and to the Nigerian seminarian who graciously allowed me to use, as chapter 7, his incisive essay on the perils and pitfalls of African inculturation. His name cannot be given due to the political climate in the Catholic Church at this time. Thanks are due as well to Matthew Frederes for re-creating one of the statistical charts. Chapter 6 first appeared at *New Liturgical Movement* on January 23, 2023, and in slightly revised form at *Rorate Caeli* on January 24; chapter 7 at *New Liturgical Movement* on August 17, 19, 25, 31, and September 1, 2022; chapter 8 at *New Liturgical Movement* on April 19, 2017; chapter 9 at *Liturgical Arts Journal* on August 3, 2022; chapter 10 at *New Liturgical Movement* on July 6, 2020; and chapter 11 at *New Liturgical Movement* on June 8, 2020. All are found here in their definitive versions.

Peter A. Kwasniewski

November 20, 2024

St. Felix of Valois

PART 1

GEORGE NEUMAYR'S ARTICLES

in

THE AMERICAN SPECTATOR

1

THE DECLINE OF CATHOLICISM ON AFRICA'S IVORY COAST

Decolonization and the liberalism of Vatican II didn't help

DECEMBER 28, 2022

I SPENT CHRISTMAS TRAVELING to the Republic of Côte d'Ivoire, Africa's Ivory Coast. A few months ago, looking around for a new project, I developed a book proposal examining the condition of Christianity on the continent of Africa and what the Western Church could learn from it, both good and bad. Whether or not I can produce such a book remains to be seen, but I am writing this column from Grand-Bassam, the old French colonial capital near Abidjan, the urban and financial center of Africa's Ivory Coast.

Toward the end of doing preliminary research on the book without spending too much money, I purchased a ticket a month or so ago using 10 years of unused travel points on my credit card. The points covered the entire trip. But I soon discovered, thanks to Dr. Fauci's COVID-based tyranny, that international travel is absurdly expensive and bureaucratic. I ended up dropping almost a grand on a negative COVID test, a yellow fever vax, and the visa. On Christmas morning, as I sat waiting for my flight to Abidjan via Brussels, I noticed to my dismay that a negative COVID test is required for entry into the Ivory Coast. So I went searching for a clinic to get one. The only clinic in Newark's airport charged $250 for the test. It was a brutal introduction to the scam that is COVID testing. I asked the mean mandarin at the desk why the test costs so much and she just shrugged indifferently. But the kicker is that I didn't even need it. After arriving in Abidjan, an aspiring Dr. Fauci at customs disregarded my negative result from the Newark clinic and demanded I submit to his test on the grounds that I am unvaccinated.

To be fair, he was the only official who gave me a hard time. Most of the "passport control" officials were easygoing, which seems to characterize the Ivory Coast's population as a whole. I had heard that West Africans are "jolly," but I wouldn't quite apply that word to the folks I have met here. They are generally well-mannered and unobtrusive, but I also notice a certain wan quality in them, as if they know that the Ivory Coast has seen better days.

Of course, it has, but one isn't supposed to notice the country's decline since France gave up its colonial presence there. That decline is manifest in the squalor of parts of Grand-Bassam, the former colonial capital which to this day retains remnants of impressive 19th-century French architecture. A visit to Grand-Bassam offers a glimpse into the glory of French culture at its best and its enchanting power. French resorts there on the Atlantic ocean capture a bit of that atmosphere.

Downtown Grand-Bassam, on the other hand, is dismal and disgusting and is vivid proof of the Ivory Coast's decline since decolonization. The most rancid neighborhood sits near a Catholic parish, which is a measure also of the Church's decline. Wouldn't a functioning Catholic parish transform such a neighborhood for the better? That clearly hasn't happened. I went into the church (called Immaculate Mary) around noon on Wednesday and found only one person praying inside. I saw a picture of Pope Francis and mused about the emptiness of his "social justice" message, evident in the fact that a Catholic parish in Grand-Bassam is no longer civilizing it.

Had I visited that parish long before Vatican II and during its traditionally French Catholic period, the neighborhood around it would not have been an open sewer, as it is today.

The combination of Vatican II's dilution of the faith and the disappearance of French colonial culture explains the fact that the Ivory

Coast today is no longer majority-Christian but majority-Muslim. It enjoys a slight majority and wears its majority status lightly, it seems to me. The Islam practiced here appears as nonthreatening as the Ivory Coast people, manifesting itself largely in colorful dresses worn by polite and modest women. One congenial woman noted to me that Islam's strength in the Ivory Coast isn't that notable given Islam's deep roots in the country. In other words, the country is reverting to its past after a Catholic interregnum.

"Social justice" Catholicism is failing everywhere, including along the Ivory Coast, where its pastors preach big government to a diminishing congregation living under shantytown conditions unimproved by socialism. Islam, to be sure, has its problems too. In 2016, Grand-Bassam witnessed a brutal Islamic terrorist attack that resulted in the deaths of 18 people. The U. S. State Department continues to warn Americans about the possibility of terrorist attacks in the country. But, frankly, I have felt fairly safe here. While I found the neighborhood near the Catholic church appalling, I didn't fear its Muslims. Abidjan and Grand-Bassam, in a way, retain the cosmopolitan character and tolerant attitudes that once flourished under the French, who introduced into this part of the world a charm that still hasn't disappeared.

2

ISLAM AND PROTESTANTISM GROW ON IVORY COAST WHILE CATHOLIC CHURCH FADES

Is it any wonder given that the country's hierarchy and clergy have diluted the faith?

DECEMBER 31, 2022

I ARRIVED ON AFRICA'S IVORY Coast on December 26. It became immediately apparent to me that Côte d'Ivoire, once a symbol of Catholicism's power to transform countries, now simply gives evidence of post-Vatican II Catholicism's decay. The country's Catholic population has fallen to 17 percent and out of that nominal group only a small percentage practice the faith regularly. Catholicism trails Protestantism and Islam. The latter enjoys influence over 40 percent of the population and is likely to keep growing, in part because the country's Islamic traditions precede French Catholicism's arrival by almost ten centuries.

At the beginning of the twentieth century, few Catholics and clergy lived on the Ivory Coast. But thanks to the noble sacrifices and fidelity of French missionaries—who came to Côte d'Ivoire preaching theology, not "social justice"—the Catholic Church soon enjoyed tremendous growth. Go back and look at press accounts from the mid-20th century and you will see reporters marveling at the Catholic faith's spread on the Ivory Coast.

But all that momentum is now gone and the Church in Côte d'Ivoire is a shadow of its former self. Today's Catholic priests offer not unvarnished Catholicism but its pitiful "social justice" variant, a blend of socialist politics, modernist theology, and ecumenical babble.

Every parish I have visited looks like a ghost town, including St. Paul's Cathedral, a modernist monstrosity in downtown Abidjan. Built in the 1980s at huge cost, the architecturally lame cathedral is difficult to describe, featuring a shapeless "African man," an allegory of some sort lost on me and many others. I walked into the vast structure—the second largest cathedral on the African continent—and not a single person was inside praying. True, one doesn't expect a huge number of Catholics inside a church on a week day. But nobody? In the second largest cathedral in Africa?

Needless to say, St. Paul would find St. Paul's Cathedral unimpressive. St. Paul preached Jesus Christ crucified, not humanist dreck. The message of the cathedral, which looks like it belongs more to the tradition of UNESCO than Catholicism, is depressingly confused and amounts to a Christianity without Christ. Who would bother to join such a feeble quasi-religion? Who would bother to keep practicing it?

The evangelicals I have met here are on fire for Jesus Christ. I was told by one that their Sunday services routinely last 5 hours—a sharp contrast to phoned-in, lackluster Catholic masses which feature hollow lectures about "social justice." It is obvious that the Catholic hierarchy here is pandering to that emphasis under Pope Francis while presiding over an institution that does almost nothing to alleviate the poverty and dysfunction that surround Catholic parishes. Every one of them I have visited sits in the midst of appalling squalor and poverty, something the pre-Vatican II French missionaries would never have tolerated. Grand-Bassam, the old French colonial capital, is now largely a pigsty, surrounded by faded Catholic parishes either unwilling or incapable of alleviating that misery.

A religion of "social justice" that can't eliminate degradation in the neighborhoods in which its parishes operate is worthless and will have no appeal. Making matters even more catastrophic for the Church is that the clergy add on top of this hypocritical and destructive socialism an "interfaith" relativism that renders membership in the Church utterly meaningless. Why would anyone on the Ivory Coast choose Catholicism over Islam or Protestantism given that its pitch is so weak and its civilizing powers so non-existent?

Before they largely left in the wake of Vatican II, French missionaries said in effect to the people of the Ivory Coast: Jesus Christ wants you to enter His Church and we will make life better for you. And they did. Life was "a lot" better under the French, a black African woman said to me the other day. This woman turned out to be a supporter of Donald Trump and readily agreed with his assessment of decolonized African countries as "s**tholes."

Unfortunately, Côte d'Ivoire falls into that category—garbage heaps across Abidjan testify to it—while retaining pockets of French charm, European industry, and native African decency. Most of the people I have met here are mellow, fairly well-mannered, and at times astonishingly kind. So even though many of them aren't Catholic anymore and wouldn't even know what the ideologically freighted phrase "social justice" means, they embody in their kindness to an isolated white man from America like me the Christian ethos the French missionaries fostered far better than any bloviating bishop dining at the

Hotel Sofitel could. The kindness I have encoun-
tered is a tribute to the best of French and
African culture that the pre-Vatican II Church
blended together so effectively for decades but
that has sadly dissipated under their modernist
successors who now preside over increasingly
empty pews.

3

THE CURIOUS STORY OF IVORY COAST'S NOTRE DAME BASILICA, AFRICA'S LARGEST CATHOLIC CHURCH

It was a billionaire's gift to the Vatican. Today, it looks like a ghost town

JANUARY 7, 2023

LAST THURSDAY AFTERNOON, I hired a driver from Yango, the Ivory Coast's version of Uber, to take me to Yamoussoukro, the political capital of Côte d'Ivoire. I wanted to see the Notre Dame Basilica, the largest Catholic church on the continent of Africa. I had already visited St. Paul's Cathedral in Abidjan, an appallingly amorphous and modernist church that looks like a committee at the United Nations designed it.

Notre Dame Basilica, on the other hand, is recognizably and impressively Catholic. It is modeled after St. Peter's Basilica in Vatican City and in fact dwarfs it in size. The dome is massive, surely the largest one on the continent of Africa if not the world. Last Friday morning, which was the feast of the Epiphany, I took a tour of the church. Earlier at my hotel, which had an Epiphany scene in its lobby, I mentioned to some staffers that I was heading over to the basilica in the hopes of finding an Epiphany Mass. They looked at me blankly. Their total ignorance of the significance of the Epiphany struck me as yet another measure of Catholicism's decline on the Ivory Coast. This cluelessness contrasts sharply with the devoutness of Muslims, whom I could hear at 5:30 in the morning chanting at a nearby mosque.

My Yango driver delivered me to the basilica, officially called Basilique Notre-Dame de la Paix, around 9. I expected to find at least a few dozen Catholics there on a day as important as the Epiphany. Instead, I walked into an empty basilica, a church that holds 18,000 within its interior and 200, 000 throughout the whole structure. It has a large square similar to St. Peter's Square, with an imitation of the famous "arms of Bernini."

It looked as much like a ghost town as St. Paul's Cathedral and made me wonder: How is it that the Ivory Coast, where Catholicism has been declining since the disappearance of French missionaries after Vatican II, boasts the two largest Catholic structures on the continent of Africa? I don't know the story behind the funding of St. Paul's Cathedral—though I suspect at least some

of it came from the globalist set in Abidjan—but
I now know the story behind the basilica's cre-
ation. It was built not by the Vatican or the local
Catholic Church but by a billionaire, Felix Boigny,
the first president of the country after French
colonial rule ended in 1960. Boigny came from
a royal tribe in Yamoussoukro that had been
converted to Catholicism by French missionaries.

Such was his gratitude to his pre-Vatican II
mentors that he decided during the pontificate of
John Paul II to build the largest Catholic church
in Africa and give it gratis to the Vatican. According to my tour guide, the land for the basilica,
which once belonged to Boigny and served as the
ground for a vast coconut plantation (coconuts
are featured in the basilica's stained glass, as is
Boigny himself) is treated by the government
as "Vatican territory," even though it doesn't
pay a penny for it. To this day, the estate of
Boigny, plus entrance fees from tourists, cover
all costs associated with the basilica's upkeep
and maintenance.

"It is a church first and a tourist attraction second," said my tour guide. The reverse looked true
to me. I saw no Catholics praying in it. But I did
see a gaggle of tourists, though not even many
of them. I asked the tour guide about the basilica's Catholic life. He told me that one Mass is
held there a day and that it only attracts around

seventy people. On Sunday, he said, attendance probably reaches around seven hundred people. In other words, the basilica is akin to a beautiful mausoleum, striking on the outside, impressive in its decorated interior, but devoid of life.

There is a statue of Pope John Paul II inside the basilica, a nod to his three visits to the Ivory Coast. The guide mentioned that two Polish priests are still on staff, but I can't imagine that they have much to do. I ran into a woke liberal French priest inside the church and chatted with him briefly. I assume the Polish priests are less flaky. But who knows? All bets are off under Pope Francis, for whom heterodoxy has become the new orthodoxy, evident in his phoned-in funeral Mass for his more traditional predecessor. The "social justice" church of Pope Francis has been a spectacular failure in Côte d'Ivoire, where it has fallen badly behind Islam and Protestantism. As one Ivorian Muslim put it to me, the Church on the Ivory Coast suffers from an addiction to "money, power, and sex" without any discernible interest in real religion. Christians with whom I have spoken, meanwhile, keep their distance from ascendant Muslims, considering them "weird."

Boigny's basilica is a tribute not to post-Vatican II Catholicism, which has proven incapable of growth, but to the orthodoxy of French missionaries who impressed upon the budding billionaire the importance of transcendent faith in Jesus Christ and his Church. The basilica gives me some hope if only because I suspect it will serve as a glorious resource for the Church in the future after the Catholic faith one day rebounds.

4

CÔTE D'IVOIRE: AT ONCE MADDENING AND CHARMING

*The country is a fascinating blend
of French and African culture*

JANUARY 11, 2023

ONE OF THE BIG LIES IN THE West is that a high quality of living requires a high cost of living. Travel to different non-Western parts of the world and you will quickly see that that is not true. Take Côte d'Ivoire, a West African country home to much ostensible Dickensian poverty. Are its citizens more unhappy, say, than the citizens of the United States? I wouldn't say so. Their cost of living is low while their quality of living in terms of happiness is probably fairly high. Since arriving in the country in late December, I have walked through appallingly dirty (by Western standards) marketplaces and neighborhoods and seen much joy on the faces of playing children and contentment among adults, many of whom are remarkably kind and easygoing. Ivorians who make pennies a day have offered me cups of coffee, part of their sandwiches, and car rides home.

I have heard African-Americans disparage African culture and speak about Africans condescendingly. Having spent some time on the Ivory Coast, which is a unique blend of French and African culture, I find that African-American chauvinism pretty ridiculous. The Ivorians I have met represent a culture far more sophisticated, dignified, and deep than anything found among elite African-Americans, most of whom gravitate to trashy culture, empty materialism, and embrace the worst of modern white culture while turning their backs on the best of African culture, which is deeply and sincerely religious.

This is not to say that Côte d'Ivoire represents a model of good governance. It obviously doesn't. In my view, it is at times hilariously dysfunctional. Last Monday, as I returned home from a café, my taxi was pulled over by armed soldiers. They demanded to see my identification and the identification of my cab driver. After I returned to the cab, they demanded from my driver a bribe of 5,000 francs, which he paid without informing me until the end of the trip. I wouldn't have paid it. I would have called the U. S. Embassy.

Calling the bluff of corrupt government officials around here can be kind of enjoyable. Most of them are hopeless clock watchers. It is customary for government employees to spend much of their workday watching French soap operas on televisions installed near their desks. To paraphrase the old Soviet adage, they pretend to work and the Côte d'Ivoire government pretends to pay them.

Since wages are low, prices are also low. I played nine holes of golf earlier this week at the Ivoire Golf Club for $8. Four-star hotels often charge less than $100. Even the luxurious Hotel Sofitel, a magnet for the cosmopolitan elite in Abidjan, is fairly affordable on off-season days.

I am not sure if this is a product of French or African culture, but Ivorians do seem to enjoy introducing difficulties into tasks that should be simple. Its taxi system is particularly maddening. "Yango," the country's version of Uber, is simply erratic: sometimes its riders show up, often they don't. And even after they do appear, the chances of them getting you to your destination without problems of one kind or another aren't particularly high. In my experience, the drivers don't show up 50 percent of the time. I hired a Yango driver to take me up to the political capital of Côte d'Ivoire, Yamoussoukro. The ride was less than smooth. The driver gunned it up there, despite the random tires, garbage, and wildlife that often appear on the highway. As he hit the gas rather maniacally, I envisioned a fiery car death after a pack of wild dogs wandered out in the road and struck our car. That didn't happen, of course, though he did strike a tire, causing me to wonder if we could complete the trip.

The driving in Abidjan is relentlessly madcap, which makes me feel as if I am in a remake of *The Pink Panther* or some other farce. I fully expect to be in a car crash soon, so I have taken to wearing my seat belt (when it works!).

Still, for all of its problems and maddening dysfunction, Côte d'Ivoire remains a fascinating place, a product of charming French culture, a charm that the natural beauty and exotic quality of the Ivory Coast magnify. I took a trip to Grand-Bassam, the colonial capital under the French, to look at its faded but impressive architecture. I felt a bit like Martin Sheen's character in *Apocalypse Now*, a soldier who travels up a river in Vietnam and discovers on the way an aristocratic French plantation frozen in time. Grand-Bassam gives off that vibe. Amidst appalling poverty, the city still features French homes, villas, administrative buildings, and resorts that recall the grandeur of the French colonial empire.

I am told by political observers that today's French are cynically picking the economic bones of the country under the patronage of its American-educated, IMF-friendly president, Alassane Ouattara, who comes off a bit like a

Bond villain. (He keeps extending his time in office questionably.) Nevertheless, it is in good part to the French that Ivorians owe their pleasant way of life, which draws upon the French genius for forming an appealing universal culture in which a low cost of living can still translate into a high quality of life.

5

WHY ARE THE EVANGELICALS EATING THE CHURCH'S LUNCH IN CÔTE D'IVOIRE?

*It is because they are more
Catholic than the Catholics*

JANUARY 14, 2023

L AST FRIDAY NIGHT, I attended as a journalist an all-night evangelical prayer service in Abidjan, Côte d'Ivoire. The event lasted from 10 p.m. on Friday night and ended at 5 a.m. on Saturday morning. Attending the event proved very useful to my study of religions in Côte d'Ivoire. It illustrated for me that evangelicals are flourishing in large part because they cleave to a traditional, Biblical Christian spirituality that the Catholic Church under Pope Francis has abandoned. To put it as simply as possible, the evangelicals are more Catholic than the Catholics.

The fervor I saw on display at it was staggering. Unlike equivocating Catholic bishops, whose lackluster liturgies define the archdiocese of Abidjan, there is no question that the evangelicals believe passionately in the divinity of Jesus Christ. To them, he is exactly what the Nicene Creed says: God from God, light from light, true God from true God.

As FrancisChurch grows more secularized and confused, the evangelicals deepen their faith in Jesus Christ through hours of singing, prayer, and dancing. I normally don't like noisy prayer services, but I could tolerate this one in part because the performances were so good. The quality of the singing was consistently high. Say what you want about this colorful form of worship, it clearly comes from a place of selfless worship, not tedious self-indulgence. The post–Vatican II Church is notorious for its hideously lame singing and dancing that flow from a diminution of belief in Catholic orthodoxy.

Two weeks ago, I went to Mass at St. Paul's Cathedral in downtown Abidjan—a "futurist" and "humanist" church St. Paul, who preached Jesus Christ crucified, would have been the first to deplore. The church is almost a parody of anti-Catholic Masonic architecture, and it turns out the Italian architect, Aldo Spirito, belongs to a Rotarian group in Rome, which is an off-shoot of Freemasonry. His church features an enormous shapeless statue that he calls "African Man." In other words, the church honors man more than God and leaves most authentic seekers of the triune God cold. The church can

hold 5,000 Catholics, but most of its Masses
are poorly attended. At the Sunday Mass to
which I went, I saw maybe 700 Catholics tops.
I had to laugh at the defective air condition-
ing during the Mass in a structure that cost
untold millions. Is that the cathedral's way of
meeting the *Laudato si'* global warming goals
of Pope Francis?

One wonders who put up the money for
the vast church. Did the Freemasons contribute
to it? Freemasonry has bedeviled the Catholic
Church on the Ivory Coast for decades. The
French secularists brought the godless heresy
to the country in 1930, establishing a lodge
in Abidjan. For decades, the Catholic bishops
tolerated "dual membership" among "Catholic
Freemasons." Only within the last decades have
they spoken against Freemasonry, and that is
due to the bad PR it has caused the Church: it
emerged that a prominent lodge master received
Communion for years with the knowledge of
Ivory Coast's hierarchy. After that came out, the
bishops had no choice but to deny the man a
public funeral.

As Freemasons got stronger and stronger in
the country, they were condemned not by the
Catholics but by Protestants in general and Pentecostal preachers in particular. Whatever you want
to say about the theology of evangelicalism, it is

not rooted in the Christ-denying humanism of woke theologians under Bergoglio. Those theologians are peddling what St. Paul would have called a Christianity without Christ.

It turns out I stayed for almost all of the spirited event and even spoke at it. A pastor asked me to make a few remarks. I highlighted the importance of all Christians responding to Jesus Christ's call that the Gospel be spread to all the "ends of the earth." Jesus Christ didn't say some of them. He said *all* of them, including Muslim ones, of which the Ivory Coast is increasingly an obvious example, with its ascendant Islam. The crowd responded to my remarks warmly and the kindly pastor reaffirmed them after I sat down. He said that love of our Muslim brothers and sisters should lead us to present the Gospel to them, not because we hate them, but because we love them and want them to enjoy eternal salvation and complete joy in Jesus Christ.

In truth, loud church events usually annoy me. But this one passed quickly and provided me with a clear picture of why evangelicals and other Protestants, which have eclipsed the Church in numbers, are eating the Catholic Church's lunch in the country. As Jesus Christ told the first bishops, human beings want bread, not stones. The evangelicals are offering that substance based on the Nicene Creed to them, at the very moment most of the bishops reveal doubts about it. Of the 17 percent of Catholics in the country, very few practice the faith consistently, whereas the evangelicals devote their Sundays and even astonishingly long Friday services to glorifying the Son of God.

PART II

CORRECTING A
MISLEADING NARRATIVE

6

IS AFRICAN CATHOLICISM A "VATICAN II SUCCESS STORY"?

PETER KWASNIEWSKI

AN EPISODE OF "WORD ON Fire" responded with two arguments to a pair of Ross Douthat articles on the failure of Vatican II.[1] Argument #1: To blame the collapse of Catholicism in the West on Vatican II is a "post hoc propter hoc" fallacy. Argument #2: The growth of the Church in Africa since Vatican II is entirely thanks to The Council. (It hardly requires pointing out that the second argument commits the same logical fallacy.)

Nevertheless, this oft-repeated claim about Africa really deserves to be examined more closely, as it is one of the great myths of our time.

> In Africa, touted most frequently as a "Vatican II success," the number of Catholics receiving the sacraments per 1000 also collapsed after

---

[1] See Ross Douthat, "How Catholics Became Prisoners of Vatican II" and "How Vatican II Failed Catholics—and Catholicism," in Peter A. Kwasniewski, ed., *Sixty Years After: Catholic Writers Assess the Legacy of Vatican II* (Brooklyn, NY: Angelico Press, 2022), 63–73.

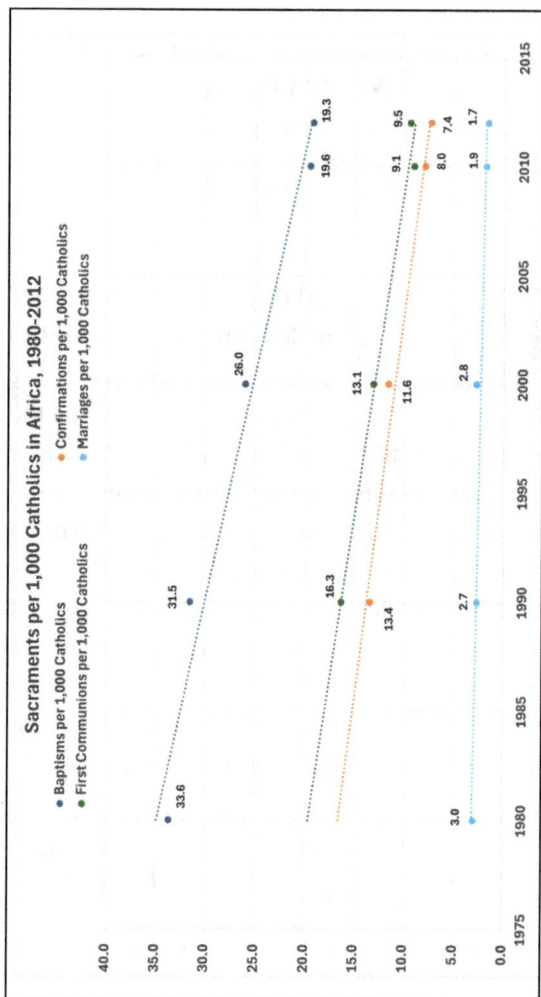

Sacraments per 1,000 Catholics in Africa, 1980-2012

● Baptisms per 1,000 Catholics   ● Confirmations per 1,000 Catholics
● First Communions per 1,000 Catholics   ● Marriages per 1,000 Catholics

Vatican II, as this chart [opposite] indicates[2] (interestingly, it seems that CARA [Center for Applied Research in the Apostolate] has removed the study from their own website, without explanation, although it was reported on widely at the time).[3]

Mr Casey continued:

In 1900 Catholics were 2% of the total African population. By Vatican II, that had ↑ to 13%. After Vatican II, the number's been nearly stagnant: ~16%, paling in comparison to Prots, whose % doubled during that time, 15% → 29%. The "Catholics" ↑ = b/c the population tripled. "But that [post-Vatican II] growth is primarily due to a higher birth rate, 'not to conversion or evangelization,' observed Fr. Thomas Reese, social scientist & columnist for NCR." "CARA: the growth can be attributed to high fertility rates . . ."[4]

---

[2] Chart is from Cathy Lynn Grossman, "More Catholics, fewer receiving sacraments: A new report maps a changing church," *Religion News Service*, June 1, 2015.

[3] https://twitter.com/MrCasey62/status/161320312807319 1426.

[4] See https://twitter.com/MrCasey62/status/1613203131567 071235; Grossman, "More Catholics, fewer receiving sacraments," referencing Thomas Reese, "Global Catholic population up, number of priests down since 1980," *National Catholic Reporter*, June 1, 2015.

Another interesting graph:[5]

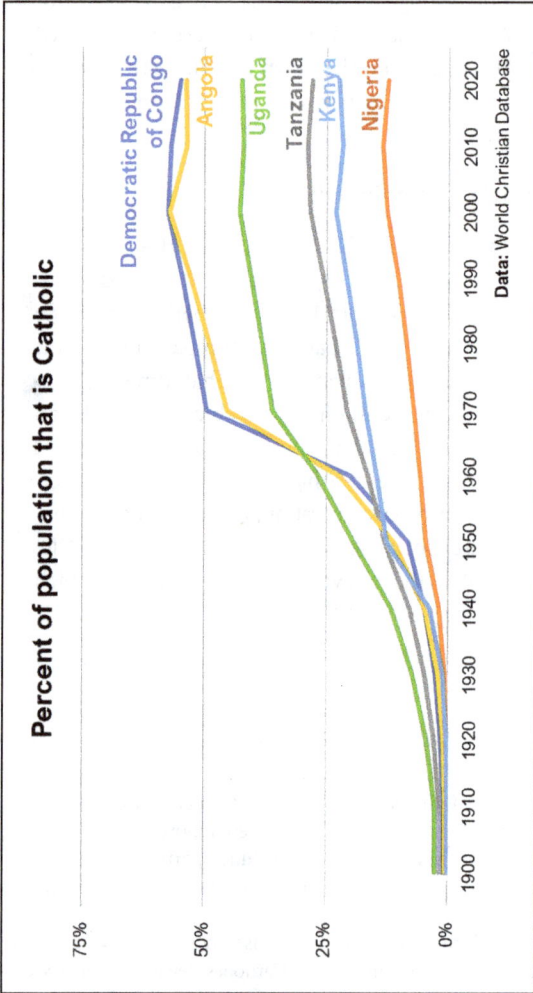

Percent of population that is Catholic

Democratic Republic of Congo · Angola · Uganda · Tanzania · Kenya · Nigeria

Data: World Christian Database

[5] Brendan Hodge, "Demography reigns down in Africa," *The Pillar,* December 29, 2021.

This graph, too, tells its own tale:

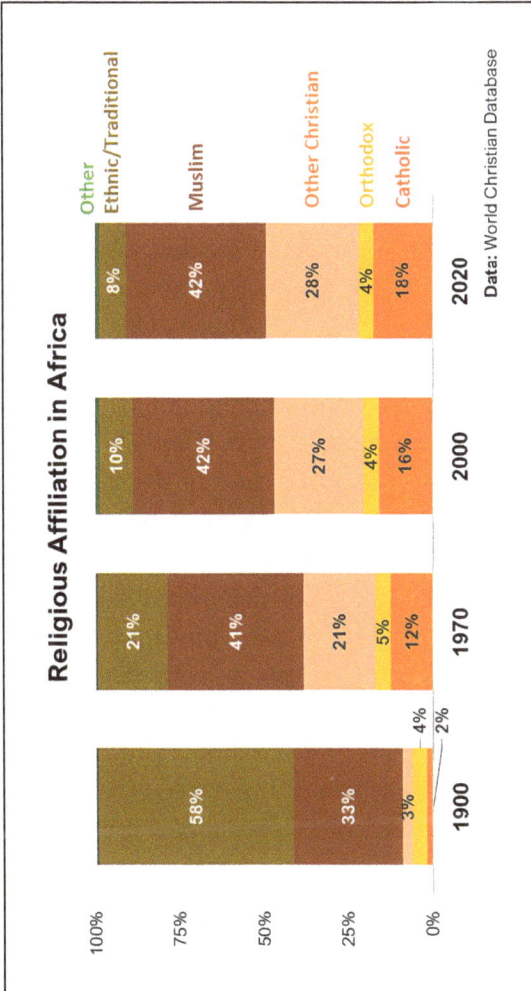

Religious Affiliation in Africa

	Other	Ethnic/Traditional	Muslim	Other Christian	Orthodox	Catholic
1900		58%	33%	3%	4%	2%
1970		21%	41%	21%	5%	12%
2000		10%	42%	27%	4%	16%
2020		8%	42%	28%	4%	18%

Data: World Christian Database

About this graph, someone online commented:

> The 600% increase in Catholics in Africa to 1970
> has been followed by a 50% increase since. What,
> I wonder, caused the inflection in the graph?
> Oh right: the counterfactual that "it would have
> been worse" had the Council never...

George Neumayr, the investigative journalist whose death in Africa shocked the Catholic
world, was in Ivory Coast working on a book
on the state of the local Church. One can read
on his Twitter feed, from December 26 to January 15, some initial impressions. For example,
concerning the photo on the opposite page, he
remarks: "Here is a picture of the 9am Mass
at St. Paul's Cathedral in Abidjan. I spoke to
the presiding priest before Mass. He was in
complete denial about the crisis and said that
Islam is only stronger than Christians because of
'immigrants.'"[6] On January 13, he tweeted: "As the
Freemasons got stronger and stronger on the Ivory
Coast, they were condemned not by Catholic bishops but by Pentecoastal preachers. The bishops
only weakly criticized them out of embarrassment
after it came out that the head of a Masonic lodge
had been receiving Communion."[7] The present

[6] https://twitter.com/george_neumayr/status/161457712295
7197316.
[7] https://twitter.com/george_neumayr/status/161401789521
7913856.

book includes the series of five articles George published at *The American Spectator,* enlightening though depressing, about the downfall of Catholicism in Côte d'Ivoire; parallels can be seen in other parts of postconciliar Africa.

In their article-series at *Church Life Journal*, Drs. Cavadini, Healy, and Weinandy commit the error of "African exceptionalism" when they write: "Across the continent of Africa, for example, celebrations of the Mass that are both vibrant and reverent attract thousands of people to the Church."[8] The assessment of Mass in Africa as "vibrant and reverent" seems to be true as far as it goes, but why should this be attributed to the celebrations rather than to Christ Himself who draws people to the Church? After all, *before* the imposition of the Novus Ordo, it was the traditional Latin Mass that fostered, or at least did nothing to prevent, the conversion of Africans to Catholicism, during the period in which the Church saw its most spectacular growth on the continent. I suspect anyone visiting *those* Masses back then would also have noted the reverence and joy.

Archbishop Marcel Lefebvre was a missionary in Africa from 1932–1959 and oversaw an astonishing spread of Catholicism in the regions of Africa for which he was responsible, which came to include twelve archdioceses, thirty-six

---

[8] John Cavadini, Mary Healy, and Thomas Weinandy, "The Way Forward from the Theological Concerns with the TLM Movement," *Church Life Journal*, November 23, 2022. For commentary, see Janet E. Smith, "Unity, Charismatic Masses, and Africa," in Peter A. Kwasniewski, *Illusions of Reform: Responses to Cavadini, Healy, and Weinandy in Defense of the Traditional Mass and the Faithful Who Attend It* (Lincoln, NE: Os Justi Press, 2023), 41–45.

dioceses, and thirteen Italian Apostolic Prefectures. No one should be surprised to discover that the TLM parishes in Africa today are flourishing, as the third episode of *The Mass of the Ages* trilogy so movingly showed. Clearly, changing the liturgy was unnecessary on this continent. Just like everyone else on the globe, Africans, too, since Vatican II, have been denied something that had already been an appreciated part of their Catholic life and heritage. There is every indication that African Catholics, like so many believers in the West, would flock to the TLM were it made more available to them. The lack of its availability can hardly then be used as an argument against its appeal or power of attraction.

Here it is not inopportune to mention that the notion of an "inculturated" African liturgy was not the work of Africans themselves but of European experts imaginatively conjuring up the "spirit" of their southern brethren—a topic taken up at length in the next chapter.

Any honest examination of the state of Catholicism in the "global south" must include reference to the fact that, while Catholicism is growing in *absolute* numbers due to population growth, Protestant and Pentecostal sects are experiencing much higher *rates of growth*— and tragically, attracting fallen-away Catholics into their numbers. This does not sound like an unmitigated "success story." Notably, the growth rate of Catholicism in Africa was proportionately much higher *prior* to 1970—that is, at the tail end of the "Tridentine" period.[9] In short, the African Church is growing simply because the population is growing (since Africans largely want to have families, unlike the trend in Western nations), so there are more Catholics in absolute numbers than sixty years ago; but the *rate of growth* is dramatically less today than it was prior to the Council. The conclusion is unavoidable: if Vatican II was supposed to be not just about maintaining the status quo of the 1950s but about launching a new evangelistic and missionary expansion, it failed in Africa, as it did everywhere else, compared to the old-fashioned approach followed over the preceding century.

What we are seeing with claims of African exceptionalism, a myth called into question by the facts, is very similar to what we see in nearly every discussion of the glories or successes of Vatican II or of the liturgical reform that followed it: namely, a willingness either to ignore evidence or, possibly, even to twist the truth for ideological reasons.

---

[9] See the Pew Research Center, "Overview: Pentecostalism in Africa," October 5, 2006, www.pewresearch.org/religion/ 2006/10/05/overview-pentecostalism-in-africa/. For further considerations on the question of missionary expansion, see chapter 10 below.

7
INCULTURATION: A WRONG TURN

BY A NIGERIAN CATHOLIC

INTRODUCTION AND BACKGROUND

O N THE FIRST SUNDAY OF Advent in 2019, Pope Francis celebrated Mass for the Congolese community in Rome at St. Peter's Basilica using the Zaire Usage of the Roman Rite. A news piece published on several outlets, "Joyous Congolese dances, songs enliven St. Peter's Basilica,"[1] reported the event at the time. The report did not fail to contrast the scenes of jubilation and dance "with the solemnity of most religious ceremonies at the Vatican." The Zaire Usage is said to stand on the summit of the program of liturgical adaptation ushered in by Vatican II.[2]

Other than the cheerful swaying, waving, and dancing to rhythmical music, which many have considered the genuine characteristic of African

---

[1] Frances D'Emilio, "Joyous Congolese Dances, Songs Enliven St. Peter's Basilica," *Voice of America*, English news, December 1, 2019, story by Associated Press.

[2] Nathan P. Chase, "A History and Analysis of the *Missel Romain pour les Dioceses du Zaire*," *Obsculta* vol. 6, no. 1 (2013): 28–36.

religious experience, in contrast to the more
sombre traditional Catholic liturgical piety, the
Zaire Usage exhibits other novelties, of which the
most contentious has been the invocation and
veneration of *ancestors*. Who may become an
ancestor, what sort of power is exerted by these
ancestors, and what does it mean (objectively
and subjectively) to venerate them are some of
the persistent questions which are not readily
answered. One author has described the ancestors as "the wise, brave and old parents (men
and women) who in the time of their human
existence have brought honor to their families
and descendants."[3] Another related various opinions on the power and influence of ancestors
on the living.[4] Perhaps because ancestors are
variously understood, the Congolese Episcopal
Conference limited the ancestors invoked in the
Zairean Use to those "of the right heart, which
are under the merits of Christ."[5]

The defenders of the doctrine of the "invocation of ancestors" are generally unwilling to
reconcile the "ancestors of the right mind" with
the saints as one would think of them on All
Saints' Day. Rather, they content themselves with

---

[3] C. N. Egbulem, quoted by Chase, "History and Analysis."
[4] Anthony Chiorazzi, "The Spirituality of Africa," *The Harvard Gazette*, October 6, 2015.
[5] Chase, "History and Analysis."

merely justifying the cult of ancestors alongside the cult of the saints and in so doing signify a divide between the two.[6] Once the ancestors are in fact separated from the saints, the justification for the former, built on the latter, becomes shaky; the two prove to be at odds. For instance, whereas Christ, "the firstborn of every creature,"[7] is the first in the line of saints, for some He does not even qualify as an ancestor, since only those who "died at a ripe-old age"[8] and were not "cursed by the gods" as to die young[9] can be so regarded.[10] Are traditional African societies not broadminded enough to honour not only their elders but also their heroes and achievers, whatever their age?

At least one African scholar, John S. Mbiti, claims for dead African children and young adults reverence from the living.[11] Chinua Achebe, in his critically acclaimed fictional work, *Things*

---

[6] Ibid.

[7] Colossians 1:15.

[8] Francis O. C. Njoku, "Some Indigenous Models in African Theology and an Ethic of Inculturation," *Bulletin of Ecumenical Theology*, vol. 8, no. 2 (1996): 4–32, at 10.

[9] A. S. O. Okwu, "Life, Death, Reincarnation, and Traditional Healing in Africa," *Issue: A Journal of Opinion*, vol. 9, no. 3 (1979): 19–24.

[10] Njoku, "Some Indigenous Models," 10–11.

[11] Innocent C. Onyewuenyi, "A Philosophical Reappraisal of African Belief in Reincarnation," *Présence Africaine*, new series, vol. 123 (1982): 63–78; the same article was published in vol. 22 of the *International Philosophical Quarterly*.

Fall Apart, a tragic novel renowned for its fidelity to the authentic habits and customs of the Igbo people before and during the early days of European colonization, informs us that Africans are not invariably ageists. "Age was respected among his people [the Igbos], but achievement was revered. As the elders said, if a child washed his hands he could eat with kings."[12]

We will have reasons to return to *Things Fall Apart* in the course of this discussion, but for the moment it is worth noting that Achebe and Mbiti squarely contradict those who insist on an Africanism in which long life is the necessary basis for venerability. Such a narrow mind-set is obviously at variance with revealed Truth.[13]

When controversies surrounding reincarnation, whether it is nominal,[14] partial,[15] or full,[16] and how these conflicting beliefs intersect the ancestral cult are brought to the fore, the rite of the "veneration of ancestors" in the Zaire

---

[12] Chinua Achebe, *Things Fall Apart* (New York: Anchor Book, 1994), 8.

[13] For example: "For venerable old age is not that of long time, nor counted by the number of years: but the understanding of a man is grey hairs. And a spotless life is old age... Being made perfect in a short space, he fulfilled a long time" (Wisdom 4:8,9,13).

[14] B. Stefaniszyn, "African Reincarnation Re-examined," *African Studies*, vol. 13, nos. 3–4 (1954): 131–46.

[15] Onyewuenyi, "Philosophical Reappraisal."

[16] Okwu, "Life, Death, Reincarnation."

Usage or other proposed revisions of the Roman Rite become even more disconcerting. In this respect, the words of our Lord to the Samaritan woman, "You adore that which you know not,"[17] takes on a new and pressing significance. I shall attempt to show further on that the "veneration of ancestors," though the most concerning doctrinal innovation in the Zairean Use, is not the only problem that arises from inculturation as understood and practiced in the Church today. In order to do this effectively, I will briefly evaluate the root, nature, and the fruits of Catholic inculturation in recent times.

Liturgical adaptation in Vatican II

Vatican II is credited with laying the foundation in the Catholic Church of inculturation as the term is understood today,[18] although the term did not occur in any document of the council. *Sacrosanctum Concilium* of Vatican II, while stipulating the revision of liturgical books, provided "for legitimate variations and adaptations to different groups, regions, and peoples, especially in mission lands, provided that the

---

[17] John 4:22.
[18] Edward Inyanwachi, "A Content Analysis of Church Documents Relative to the Role of Catholic Schools and Universities in Nigeria in the Process of Inculturation," Doctoral Thesis, University of San Francisco (2007), 6.

substantial unity of the Roman rite is preserved"
while envisaging an "even more radical adaptation of the liturgy."[19] The promulgation of the
Novus Ordo Missae and the liturgical adaptation
enjoined by *Sacrosanctum Concilium* and extolled
by Paul VI were quickly implemented all over
the world. This led to the almost complete disappearance of the immemorial Traditional Latin
Mass, and the disuse of the Latin language and
Gregorian Chant in favour of local languages
and native music. The widespread adoption of
elements of local piety and festivities, including
dancing and clapping as well as popular music
cultures such as afrobeat, rock, and yé-yé soon
became normative in different parts of the
world.[20] In addition, liturgical and disciplinary
abuses of a more grave nature were not uncommon.[21] These liturgical novelties were justified
on the ground that they lead to the "full and
active participation by all the people" in the
liturgical life of the Church, which *Sacrosanctum*

---

[19] Vatican II, *Sacrosanctum Concilium*, nos. 38 and 40.

[20] Duncan Wielzen, "Popular Religiosity and Roman Liturgy:
Toward a Contemporary Theology of Liturgical Inculturation
in the Caribbean," Doctoral Thesis, Katholieke Universiteit
Leuven (2009), 35–37.

[21] Dennis M. Doyle, "The Concept of Inculturation in Roman
Catholicism: A Theological Consideration," Religious Studies
Faculty Publications (2012), 102, https://ecommons.udayton.
edu/rel_fac_pub/102.

Concilium held as the "aim to be considered before all else."[22] Nevertheless, the celebration of the Novus Ordo in the more reverent style of the traditional Catholic liturgies continued in some places.

Adaptation outdated and inculturation extolled

Although the program of liturgical adaptation formulated in *Sacrosanctum Concilium* was welcomed enthusiastically and implemented optimistically across the Catholic world, its provisions have since been declared too restrictive and inadequate for modern evangelization. Many have voiced their dissatisfactions with the alleged superficial impact of liturgical adaptation allowed by *Sacrosanctum Concilium*, which they claim only incorporated certain local symbols and practices in the liturgy, but left the cultural depth of the people unengaged.[23] Consequently, they opted for the policy of inculturation, which has been widely described as the "incarnation" of the Gospel into a particular cultural context, and touted as the effective scheme for the evangelization of

---

[22] *Sacrosanctum Concilium*, no. 14.

[23] Wielzen, "Popular Religiosity and Roman Liturgy," 178–79; George C. Nche, Lawrence N. Okwuosa, Theresa C. Nwaoga, "Revisiting the Concept of Inculturation in a Modern Africa: A Reflection on Salient Issues," *HTS Teologiese Studies/Theological Studies*, vol. 72, no. 1 (2016), a3015.

modern societies.[24] The process of inculturation
is said to involve "the Christianization of culture
and the culturing of Christianity."[25]

The popularity of inculturation seems to
stem from its advocacy of a two-way traffic of
influence between the universal Church and a
local culture, such that the Gospel does not only
permeate and transform the culture in question, but is itself permeated and enriched by the
culture. To realize this outcome, proponents of
inculturation insist on a "dialogue" between the
Church and particular cultures exercised on the
firm grounds of reciprocity.[26] That is, the Church
must be ready and willing to be transformed as
much as she is eager to transform the cultures
of the people she evangelizes. In the same way
Paul VI sanctioned liturgical adaptation, John
Paul II gave his support for the inculturation
of "the whole of Christian existence —theology,
liturgy, customs, structures" on the condition
that nothing that is "of divine right" or an ele-
ment of "the great discipline of the Church" is
compromised.[27]

---

[24] Fiona Bowie, "The Inculturation Debate in Africa," *Studies
in World Christianity*, vol. 5, no. 1 (2011): 67–92; Wielzen,
"Popular Religiosity and Roman Liturgy," 180–82, 184–85.

[25] Wielzen, 186.

[26] Wielzen, 186–87.

[27] John Paul II, *Ecclesia in Africa*, §78.

Conditions of inculturation ignored

There are already troubling signs in some quarters that the condition for inculturation demanded by the pope has gone unheeded. Some Catholics are now openly calling for the syncretization of the Roman Liturgy with religious elements borrowed from non-Christian religions,[28] and there is even a scholarly paper that claimed, approvingly, that such syncretic worship is a regular feature of a particular Catholic parish in Nigeria.[29] I would have been inclined to dismiss such an account as altogether improbable if not for a similar incident closer to home. The parish priest of my village in Nigeria stirred much apprehension and confusion some years ago when he publicly advocated for Catholics to return to elements of the traditional non-Christian religion. He followed this general invitation away from the Catholic Faith with a call for practitioners of the local Traditional African Religion to participate in the life of the Church without renouncing practices and opinions incompatible with the

---

[28] Njoku, "Some Indigenous Models"; Cajetan Anyanwu, "Reshaping the Theology and Praxis of Inculturation through Interreligious Dialogue Between the Catholic Church and African Traditional Religion in Igboland, Nigeria," Doctoral Thesis, Duquesne University (2019), 199–203, 223, 235.
[29] Frank A. Salamone and Michael C. Mbabuike, "The Plight of the Indigenous Catholic Priest in Africa: An Igbo Example," *Africa*, vol. 49, no. 2 (1994): 210–24.

Church's teaching. Only an episcopal intervention that ousted the priest in question brought the scandal to an end.

Meanwhile, some scholars are making a case for the abandonment of inculturation altogether in favour of "interculturation" because the former, they claim, "does not fully take into account the complicated reality of the interaction between Christian cultures and other cultures and religions."[30] To "discover the intercultural face of God residing in the midst of diversely constructed human cultures and religious perspectives"[31] was declared the objective of interculturation. Is this not a call for the direct embrace and approbation of the idolatrous cultus of non-Christian religions and the complete relativization of Revelation? It seems obvious that the hierarchy of the Church cannot now validate interculturation without risking a formal approval of syncretism and pantheism.

COMMON CLAIMS OF THE PROPONENTS OF INCULTURATION

Although there is an obvious disagreement on which term—adaptation, inculturation, interculturation, or some other piece of academic

[30] Bernardus A. Rukiyanto, "Interculturation as Threefold Dialogue: Learning Experience from the Church in Asia," *UTP Journals*, vol. 30, no. 2 (2007): 165–73.
[31] Grenham as quoted by Rukiyanto.

jargon—best describes the movement, supporters of the accommodation of various aspects of the life of the Church to local practices (which I will refer to interchangeably as inculturation or adaptation) are more or less in agreement on a number of points.

(1) That these reform efforts requiring the Church to prioritize direct and reciprocal engagements with particular cultures through legislations and experiments are necessary not only for the flourishing of the Church but also for its survival.[32]

(2) That such engagements constitute a return to the primitive practice of liturgical independence in the early Church, which continues to exist in Eastern rite churches.[33]

(3) That before Vatican II, the Church sanctioned and operated a largely hegemonic policy that demonized, discredited, and destroyed non-European cultures and imposed on the local

---

[32] Inyanwachi, "Content Analysis of Church Documents," 1–3, 46, 68; O. A. Alimnonu, "Review of Austin Echema, *Corporate Personality in Traditional Igbo Society and the Sacrament of Reconciliation*," *Bulletin of Ecumenical Theology*, vol. 8, no. 2 (1996): 66–69.

[33] Ikechukwu Anthony Kanu, "Inculturation and the Christian Faith in Africa," *International Journal of Humanities and Social Science*, vol. 2, no. 17 (2012): 236–44; Jorge Presmanes, "Inculturation as Evangelization: The Dialogue of Faith and Culture in the Work of Marcello Azevedo," *U. S. Catholic Historian*, vol. 30, no. 1 (2012): 59–76.

population Western principles and a Western practice of Christianity.[34] These claims deserve an appraisal.

1. The necessity of inculturation

The first assertion, the prioritization of direct and reciprocal engagement with cultures for the survival and flourishing of the Church, has been repeated in documents of episcopal conferences and scholarly publications, although no data has ever been adduced for its substantiation. Maybe that is because all available data seem to prove the opposite, namely, that inculturation is destroying, rather than promoting, the Catholic Faith. For instance, as liturgical adaptation is energetically implemented in the Catholic world, the global number of Catholics fell below the population of Muslims for the first time in history.[35] Detailed statistical data on every measurable aspect of Catholic life in the US, Canada, and some European countries showed a precipitous decline following the policies of rapprochement with contemporary cultures and sensibilities in the wake

---

[34] Presmanes, "Inculturation as Evangelization"; Inyanwachi, "Content Analysis of Church Documents," 4, 20, 31; Njoku, "Some Indigenous Models."

[35] "Vatican: Islam Surpasses Roman Catholicism as World's Largest Religion," Associated Press, March 30, 2008, www.foxnews.com/story/vatican-islam-surpasses-roman-catholicism-as-worlds-largest-religion.

of Vatican II.[36] The significant inroads made by various Protestant groups in Catholic Latin America on the heels of widespread liturgical adaptation and the ascendency of Liberation Theology clearly shows that the Catholic decline cannot be explained by general societal secularization.

Although today Catholicism continues to grow in sub-Saharan African countries like Nigeria, the increase is due largely to population growth, but accompanied by substantial attrition in favour of the Pentecostal branch of Protestantism. In contrast, in the years prior to inculturation when the liturgy was almost entirely in Latin, Catholics in Nigeria were witnessing a phenomenal increase "in the region of 10 per cent per year"![37] The picture that emerges from reviewing the available data is that in every part of the Catholic world, inculturation has been associated with abysmal decline in Catholic vigour.

2. Identification of today's inculturation with the practice of ancient Christians

The second contention, that inculturation or active liturgical adaptation today is identical with the practice of primitive Christians,

---

[36] Kenneth C. Jones, *Index of Leading Catholic Indicators: The Church since Vatican II* (Fort Collins, CO: Roman Catholic Books, 2003).

[37] René Pierre Millot, *Missions in the World Today* (New York: Hawthorn Books, 1961), 96.

can be defended only by a selective reading of
Church history, an interpretation that is even
opposed by some proponents of inculturation.[38]
As doctrines and the liturgy were spread orally
by the first Christians, it is to be expected that
improvised and non-standard liturgical formularies would be the norm. With time, liturgical
improvisations gradually morphed into structured
usages, "usages developed by slow degrees into
rites; rites expanded into"[39] more complicated
ceremonies, and finally fixed formularies were
adopted. Such an organic development in vastly
different environments is bound to introduce
much diversity in the set liturgical formularies.
The next and commonly overlooked stage of the
liturgical history is marked by unification. Smaller
Christian communities generally adopted the formularies of the great metropolitan Churches of
Rome, Antioch, Alexandria, and Constantinople.
This process continued until "the uses of Rome
and Constantinople [had] almost absorbed the
rest."[40] Thus, liturgical uniformity was favoured
not only in the West but also in the East. However, the East with a greater number of ancient

---

[38] Wielzen, "Popular Religiosity and Roman Liturgy," 192–200.
[39] Louis Duchesne, *Christian Worship: Its Origin and Evolution* (London: Society for Promoting Christian Knowledge,
1904), 54.
[40] Duchesne, 55.

sees, heterodox separate churches, and culturally alienated communities, does project a liturgical face much more diverse than the West's.

Although the Church rejoices in the diverse legitimate liturgical and disciplinary traditions that Providence has engendered in her bosom, it is not expedient for her to go about actively seeking to create more diversities in her liturgies and disciplines, any more than a multilingual country proud of the diverse tongues of her citizens will necessarily benefit if she goes out of her way to create new languages. If left to its ordinary course, i.e., if communication is unimpeded, nature will produce uniformity in a body, whether this concerns heat in a piece of metal or the dialects in England or the liturgical traditions in a Western or Eastern ecclesiastical province. Such unity flows not only from the exigencies of nature but also from the Providence of the God of nature.[41] We may thus begin to appreciate how unnatural and contrived rampant inculturation and liturgical adaptations are in a world that now practically exists as a "global village."[42]

However strong the natural case for uniformity is, and however congenial it is for the wellbeing

---

[41] John 10:16.
[42] Nche, Okwuosa, Nwaoga, "Revisiting the Concept of Inculturation"; Doyle, "The Concept of Inculturation in Roman Catholicism," 102.

of a polity, the Church at no time in her history countenanced a blanket condemnation of
liturgical diversity. When it is for the benefit of
souls, the Church has been willing to sanction
deviations from her normal liturgical practice.
We see this clearly in the story of the saintly
brothers, Sts. Cyril and Methodius, the Apostles
of the Slavs. Unfortunately, this historical event is
often erroneously presented as an example and
justification for liturgical diversity understood as
a good in its own right.[43] Nothing could be further from the intention of these apostolic brothers, as St. Cyril's defense of his actions before
the pope showed. "When I was unable to help
those people with the salvation of their souls
in another way, God inspired me through this
means, by which I have won a great many of
them for Him."[44] Clearly, St. Cyril understands
that liturgical and disciplinary adaptation is the
exception that may sometimes be helpful, rather
than the rule that must always be followed.[45]

---

[43] Wielzen, "Popular Religiosity and Roman Liturgy," 201–3.

[44] Marvin Kantor, "A Brief Account of Saints Cyril and Methodius and the Baptism of the Moravian and Bohemian Lands,"
cited in Norman E. Thomas, ed., Classic Texts in Mission and
World Christianity (New York: Orbis Books, 1995), 12.

[45] The narration continued, showing Rome's openness to
diversity when a just cause exists: "Hearing this and mar-
velling at the faith of this great man, they [the papacy] now
decreed in an apostolic decision and confirmed in writing
that the Mass and other canonical hours be sung in those

Even after the codification of disciplines
enacted by the Council of Trent and right up
to the eve of Vatican II, the Church granted dis-
pensations from her established liturgical norms
in favour of local customs when she judged such
concessions beneficial for the salvation of souls.[46]
Hence, at no time in her history did the Church
foreclose beneficial adaptations of her liturgies
and disciplines; but the pursuit of adaptations
and diversities in everything and everywhere as
a rule to be invariably followed is novel.

3. Hostility to non-European cultures

The third affirmation, the alleged hostility of
the Church to non-European cultures before
Vatican II, has many troubling and distorted sides
to it, not the least its uncharitable generalization
and ingratitude for the missionaries who left all
they cherished and gave all and themselves for the
salvation of strangers. It is easy today to lose sight

---

regions in the [Slavic] language . . . " Kantor, in Thomas,
Classic Texts in Mission, 12.

[46] Examples of such concessions include "the use of vernacular Rituals" in Asia and Africa, "the celebration of the Mass
in the literary language of China," "the right to sing the Kyrie,
Gloria, Credo and other chants of the Ordinary or the Mass
in the common language" of certain dioceses of Asia and
Africa, re-reading of Scriptural text in the vernacular at Mass,
transfer of processions to more appropriate local times, and
the "development of native religious music." Millot, *Missions
in the World Today*, 57–59.

of the enormous sacrifice a nineteenth-century European missionary made in leaving the comfort and security of home for the uncertainties of life and death, say, in a tropical jungle in Nigeria infested with malaria. There and elsewhere he must set himself not only to cure spiritual ills but also to treat the bodies and educate the minds of children and adults, even when the vast majority of the beneficiaries are not Christians.[47]

The many today that charge these missionaries and the hierarchy that directed them with insensitivity to the culture and people evangelized, cannot account for the sacrifices and achievements of these missionaries and the papal teachings of the time that guided them. For instance, Pius XII is on record instructing the missionary to "consider the country he is going to evangelize as a second fatherland and love it with due charity."[48] The pope continued:

> For the Church, when she calls people to a higher culture and a better way of life, under the inspiration of the Christian religion, does not act like one who recklessly cuts down and uproots a thriving forest. No, she grafts a good scion upon the wild stock that it may bear a crop of more delicious fruit.[49]

---

[47] Millot, 63–76.

[48] Pius XII, *Evangelii Praecones* (1951), no. 20.

[49] *Evangelii Praecones*, no. 56.

Similar exhortations for missionaries to love the people they evangelize and to respect, build on, and harness for good their culture and heritage were issued by Benedict XV, Pius XI, and John XXIII, all before Vatican II,[50] and following in the ancient trail of St. Gregory I.[51] Therefore, the common accusation of systemic utter disregard and contempt for the cultures of native populations often hurled at missionaries who laboured for the Faith before Vatican II is without merit and in bad taste.[52]

CULTURE MISUNDERSTOOD

The second quotation from Pius XII above underscores an important fact about culture too often confused. Since each culture was developed under more or less unique circumstances to solve human problems within a given context, no two cultures are wholly comparable. In this respect, no one culture is better than

---

[50] Millot, *Missions in the World Today*, 12–28.
[51] Warren H. Carroll, *The Building of Christendom* (Front Royal, VA: Christendom College Press, 1987), 198–99.
[52] Of course, it does not then follow that all missionaries before Vatican II were saints or were faultlessly prudent. Being only human, they were imperfect and may not have been entirely immune from the nationalism of their day; hence the papal injunctions on the matter (Millot, *Missions in the World Today*, 22). By and large, however, these missionaries deserve better than the common label of ethnocentric imperialists given to them.

another.[53] However, if we look upon culture as
civilization or human achievement, "that total
process of human activity and that total result
of such activity," then one culture may be more
advanced or civilized than another.[54] It should
be noted that a more advanced culture is not
the inevitable consequence of the higher intel-
ligence of a particular people relative to another
group. Civilization grows largely by "the diffusion
of cultural traits," i.e., the borrowing of ideas
and techniques by one group from other groups,
which depends on the accident of opportunities
(or, speaking more correctly, Providence) and the
willingness to assimilate.[55] The Church in building Christian civilization drew from the greatest
achievements of civilized Asia, Africa, and Europe,
which she harmonized and elaborated by the
principles of revealed truth.[56]

Hence, it is genuinely retrogressive and delete-
rious both to the Church's mission and the civilization of non-European communities to place the
Church, even with respect to her human elements,

[53] Ruth Benedict, "The Growth of Culture," in *Man, Culture,
and Society*, ed. H. L. Shapiro (New York: Oxford University
Press, 1956), 188–89.
[54] H. Richard Niebuhr, *Christ and Culture* (New York: Harper
& Row, 1951), 32–33.
[55] Benedict, "Growth of Culture," 188–92.
[56] Ildefonso Schuster, *The Sacramentary* (London: Burns,
Oates & Washbourne, 1924), vol. 1, p. 3.

on the same level as every culture of the world, however primitive. Sadly, there are some who in their effort to promote inculturation demand that the Church embrace "powerlessness" by denying her civilizing power and heritage among nations,[57] while others hold that non-European communities should as a rule prefer their own cultures to the traditional norms and practices of the Church. In other words, these communities are being asked to re-invent the wheel, to evolve from a more or less disordered foundation a process the Church has long completed and perfected—as far as completion and perfection go this side of heaven.

COMMON ASSUMPTIONS ABOUT INCULTURATION

Having completed our short overview of the propositions usually advanced in support of inculturation, and having seen how unfounded these assertions are, we will now briefly explore the foundations of a number of scholarly and popular assumptions connected with inculturation in general and African religiosity in particular.

Mutual enrichment

We will start off with the common talk about the "mutual enrichment" of the local and universal Church that necessarily results from

---

[57] Presmanes, "Inculturation as Evangelization."

inculturation or liturgical adaptation to particular communities. Without denying the salutary
effect of genuine liturgical adaptation and the
beauty of ordered diversity, it is important to
remind ourselves of the other reality: we cannot
have our cake and eat it too. Keeping the victual
metaphor, it is to be expected that one who has
always drunk coffee will likely contribute little to
a discussion on tea tasting. Likewise, to the extent
and in the respect that a local Church adopts a
unique practice, to that extent and in that respect
is she decoupled from the universal practice of
the Church. As discussed earlier, diversity *per se*
is not an evil; on the contrary, it may be a great
good, especially if there were legitimate grounds
for it. Nevertheless, for the wellbeing of the polity,
such deviations from the universal should be the
exceptions rather than the rule. Liturgical uniformity, on the other hand, by building a liturgical
bridge, as it were, between two or more cultures
and nations with different temperaments and
persuasions, does result in mutual enrichment
of the Church's communities, as the history of
the Church amply bears witness.

As a case in point, the Carolingian kings only
desired that their kingdom pray as Rome did, but
in their humility, they not only granted their people a share in the heritage of Rome, the principal
See of Christendom, but afforded the Gallican rite

the unique opportunity of substantially enrich-
ing the ancient Roman Use itself. The resulting
Frankish-Roman liturgy became the liturgical
and disciplinary patrimony of the Church in the
West.[58] This liturgical tradition and the associated
disciplines and principles produced Western civilization, and not the other way round.[59]

The Christian Faith as expressed in the Roman
Liturgy and discipline, in its original or hybrid
forms, has had as much efficacy in civilizing
the pagan and primitive tribes of Europe as it
could have in civilizing the pagan and primitive
tribes of Africa, if it is allowed to work its way
into the fibres of the cultures of the latter as
it did in those of the former. Unfortunately, a
hasty effort at the "Africanization" of the liturgy,
sometimes driven by ideologies antithetical to
the Faith, and often without any objective eval-
uation of the impact, has stalled the salutary
effect of the Latin heritage in Africa. A relevant
example that presents itself is the Zaire Usage's
close association with the Congolese dictator
Mobutu[60] and his aggressive and sometimes
anti-Christian cultural agenda, which included
the abandonment of his Christian name.

---

[58] Duchesne, *Christian Worship*, 102–4.
[59] Thomas E. Woods, *How the Catholic Church Built Western Civilization* (Washington, DC: Regnery Publishing, 2005).
[60] Inyanwachi, "Content Analysis of Church Documents," 70.

Liturgy and culture

The opinion that non-European liturgies are required for the preservation of non-European cultures is the second popular assumption for our examination. It is interesting to note that many Africans and other non-Europeans who clamour for an African or non-European liturgy to preserve or rescue African or other non-European cultures from Westernization, have themselves, alongside the vast majority of people living today, embraced much of all secular Western cultures—language, technology, philosophy, government, entertainment, etc. Their coldness towards, or outright rejection of, the Traditional Latin Mass and other traditional Catholic devotions deprive them of the necessary counterweight to the toxic effects of the post-Christian Western cultures they have adopted. At any rate, do we have any concrete evidence that the Latin liturgy poses any threat whatsoever to the positive culture of any nation?

We can readily examine this question with reference to a nation that has had a long Catholic history. St. Patrick's Ireland is a good candidate having always being outside the Roman Empire and its pre-Christian civilization.[61] Certainly, the Roman liturgy, for all the many centuries it was prayed in Latin by the Irish people, did not destroy

---

[61] Carroll, *The Building of Christendom*, 121.

the Irish culture; on the contrary, it nurtured it. Latin did not displace Irish, but English did.[62] In the same vein, Latin has never been a threat to the Igbo language, but English is. And this is not because English is taught in school or sometimes used in the church, but principally because Igbo is no longer spoken in many Igbo homes, no longer the mother tongue; making it the liturgical language does not help. The English language may indeed threaten the identity of the Igbo people, but post-Christian Western values, torn as it were from God and from the natural law, pose a mortal and infernal danger. A largely sentimental revitalization of traditional Igbo customs and its incorporation into the liturgy stand little chance in stemming the surging and sophisticated onslaught of the decadent West. Western culture became dysfunctional and corrosive by rejecting the traditional Catholicism that nurtured it; it can be tamed and harnessed for the well-being of any society only if it is reconnected to Holy Mother Church, its wellspring.

The roots of the traditional Catholic liturgy

The third popular assumption for consideration is really a common oversight. In the frequent discussion of inculturation today, it is evident

---

[62] D. Vincent Twomey, *The End of Irish Catholicism?* (Dublin: Veritas Publications, 2003), 52–53.

that many have lost sight of the fact that the
traditional Catholic liturgy and discipline is a
product, to the extent that it is man-made, of
societies with values and hopes much closer to
the indigenous peoples of Africa, Asia, and Latin
America than to post-Christian Western societies.
It was the product of customs that value the
family, respect life as a gift from God, dance and
clap in joy, and share the sorrow and fears of
neighbours and strangers. In an effort to identify
a distinguishing and central African value as a
basis for building a "theological model of inculturation," one African theologian claimed for
Africans the eminent exhibition of hospitality. The
apparent suggestion, perhaps, is that Europeans
are less hospitable. Another countered the prop-
osition only to advance Africans' eminent sense
of communion or "covenant" with people and
nature.[63] The individualism of modern Western
societies may de-emphasize personal responsibility
towards neighbours and strangers, but such an
unsocial disposition does not reflect the values
of the Church nor the cultures from which the
Church elaborated her liturgy and discipline.

Africanism in the liturgy

We will say something here about the ste-
reotypical association of African worship with

---

[63] Njoku, "Some Indigenous Models," 17–25.

dancing, drumming, clapping, and other bodily
gestures[64] and its alleged incompatibility with
silence, reflective prayer, and solemn forms of
singing/chanting, because these latter, it is claimed,
are religious expressions proper to Europeans.
That a form of liturgical dance is still preserved
in the ancient Abyssinian Rite of Ethiopia[65] while
nothing of that kind exists in the Latin Rite may
seem to support the common supposition that
dancing and other dramatic gestures of joy are,
in relation to the West, genuine and exclusive
African religious expressions. In reality, however,
"ritual dance was not foreign to the old European Church,"[66] and about a century after the
Ethiopian rite was fixed,[67] St. Teresa of Avila and
her nuns executed "sacred dance in the choir,
singing and clapping . . . in the Spanish way, but
with . . . holy reverence."[68]

[64] Wielzen, "Popular Religiosity and Roman Liturgy," 135;
Benedict Nwabugwu Agbo, "Inculturation of Liturgical Music
in the Roman Catholic Church of Igbo Land: A Compositional
Study," *Journal of Global Catholicism*, vol. 1, no. 2 (2017):
6–27; Anyanwu, "Reshaping the Theology and Praxis," 10–11,
199–200, 229.
[65] Csilla Fabo Perczel, "Art and Liturgy: Abyssinian Processional Crosses," *Northeast African Studies*, vol. 5, no. 1 (1983):
19–28.
[66] György Martin, "Dance Types in Ethiopia," *Journal of the
International Folk Music Council*, vol. 19 (1967): 23–27.
[67] Perczel, "Art and Liturgy."
[68] Marcelle Auclair, *Teresa of Avila* (New York: Doubleday
Image, 1959), 231–32.

As would have been the case in old Europe,
it should be noted that liturgical dance in the
Ethiopian or Coptic liturgy is a feature of certain open-air processions or celebrations recalling
the famed Davidic dance, and has no place in
the Mass. In fact, the Eucharistic sacrifice in the
Ethiopian Rite, as a sign of profound reverence,
is performed in secret, away from the gaze of
the lay faithful. This tradition is reminiscent of
the obsolete practice of dismissing catechumens
before the Eucharistic sacrifice in the Latin Rite,[69]
the widespread custom of installing iconostases
in Eastern rite churches, and, to some extent, the
discontinued mediaeval practice of setting up of
rood screens in Western churches. Consequently,
Africanism played no role in preserving in Ethiopia certain practices long outdated in the West.

The Psalmist invites all nations to clap their
hands and "shout unto God with the voice of
joy";[70] elsewhere, "let them praise his name in
choir [dance]."[71] Practising what he preached,
King David famously danced ahead of the proces-
sion of the Ark of the Covenant. His actions were
emulated down the ages by Ethiopian priests and
European nuns. However, such excited displays
are out of place in the Jewish temple worship at

---

[69] Duchesne, *Christian Worship*, 171.

[70] Psalm 46:2.

[71] Psalm 149:3.

Jerusalem, in the Jewish synagogue worship across the world (from which much of Christian Liturgy developed),[72] or during traditional Eucharistic worship in Ethiopia, Europe, and the rest of the Christian world. Just as Elijah recognized the Lord not in the commotions of a strong wind, earthquake, or fire, but in the "whistling of a gentle air" and then covered his face in reverence,[73] so Christ often went away from the crowd to a quiet place, alone or with his disciples, to pray.

The note of reverence and solemnity that characterizes the Jewish and Christian liturgies, especially when this involves direct communion with God in some shape or form, exists in various degrees in many non-Christian religions, including African Traditional Religions. In the latter, it sometimes takes the aspect of extreme secrecy, elitism, gravity, and even terror. At any rate, liturgical dance is not an African singularity but a universal phenomenon, which is however excluded from the most solemn religious activity in Judaism and Christianity, as well as in certain Traditional African Religions.

Concerning the place of silence and contemplation in African religious experience and expressions, it should be noted that every human being

---

[72] Duchesne, *Christian Worship*, 46.
[73] 3 Kings 19:11–13.

can laugh and cry, and they know the experience
that is neither crying nor laughing. Like lamenta-
tion and mirth, silence is a universal language that
cuts across cultures and creed. Everyone knows
what silence is—even the little baby that screams
at Mass intent on disrupting the quiet he or she
senses and is thrilled to pierce. It is equally true
that all human beings are capable of introspec-
tion and reflective thought. In some cultures or
civilizations, these habits are so developed that
mysticism or philosophy becomes noticeable. In
traditional sub-Saharan African cultures, medita-
tion and thought are largely employed to reach
out to the world of the spirit or to resolve pressing social and personal problems. Hence, philosophy is rather poorly developed, while mysticism
is largely better developed.

Granted, the traditional African mystical experience is different from the Catholic notion of
mysticism, but so was the mystical expression of
other uncultured nations in the distant past that
were brought under the Christian light. Hence,
I am a little embarrassed to have to argue for
a place for silence in the African culture or in
any other human culture. It is therefore not true
that the silence and sombreness of traditional
Catholic piety, especially in the Traditional Latin
Mass, is incompatible with the African temper. It
is rather condescending to hold such an opinion.

Even when singing in the vernacular, Africans do not always produce "throbbing dance music."

I vividly recall my experiences of weekday Novus Ordo Masses celebrated in Igbo in a neighbourhood village church during my undergraduate days in Nigeria. Usually, the sun was just about to rise, the church poorly lit and poorly furnished, and without drumming, clapping, or swaying, these poor villagers sang, mostly from memory and from the heart, the rich mysteries of the Faith in a simple and edifying form that has much in common with the decorum, balance, and prayerfulness of the Church's Gregorian chant.

THE ZAIRE USAGE AND FALSE AFRICANISM IN THE LITURGY

Returning to the Zaire Usage and drawing from our discussions above, we are compelled to admit that the excited singing and dancing at the Vatican on the First Sunday of Advent in 2019 that made such glowing headlines in the global media were neither a unique African religious/cultural expression nor were they the most dignified actions suitable to the Sacrifice of the Holy Mass. Dancing as a liturgical or devotional exercise has existed in many societies, African and non-African, and in several of these communities, including traditional Jewish and

Christian communities, reverence for the divine
has meant that such expression of excitement
was kept away from the most sacred action of
religion or the principal cultus. Many traditional
African religions extensively employ the emotion
of fear to elicit and maintain religious fervor.[74]
Practitioners are strictly obliged to offer sacrifice
and libation or suffer grave consequences.[75] Such
stringent obligation requires for compliance, and
confers on the associated religious service, a stern
and terrifying outlook—hence, the attitude of
"respectful distance" in dealing with the sacred
that is practiced in traditional African societies.[76]

This fact was graphically related by Chinua
Achebe in his novel *Things Fall Apart*,[77] from

---

[74] Wielzen, "Popular Religiosity and Roman Liturgy," 43.

[75] Onyewuenyi, "A Philosophical Reappraisal"; Okwu, "Life,
Death, Reincarnation."

[76] A. N. O. Ekwunife, "African Traditional Values and Formation in Catholic Seminaries of Nigeria," *Bulletin of Ecumenical
Theology*, vol. 8, no. 2 (1996): 49–65.

[77] "The Oracle was called Agbala, and people came from far
and near to consult it. They came when misfortune dogged
their steps or when they had a dispute with their neighbors.
They came to discover what the future held for them or to
consult the spirits of their departed fathers. The way into the
shrine was a round hole at the side of a hill, just a little bigger
than the round opening into a henhouse. Worshippers and
those who came to seek knowledge from the god crawled
on their belly through the hole and found themselves in a
dark, endless space in the presence of Agbala. No one had
ever beheld Agbala, except his priestess. But no one who had
ever crawled into his awful shrine had come out without the

which it is evident that nothing could be more out-of-place, even downright "sacrilegious", than a smiling and swaying worshipper, dancing to the tune of rhythmic joyful music, at a sacrifice or divination service in the shrine of Agbala or Amadioha or any of the other Alusi or deities of traditional Igbo religion.

But how, then, did the notion of lively singing and joyous dancing become so intimately connected with the religious expressions of Africans in modern times if such behaviors, in that context, are alien to the indigenous religion? We must look for the root of the rhythmic dance music not in the cultus of the African people but in their secular cultures or social tradition. In marked contrast to the petrifying scene of divination painted by Achebe, his description of a village wrestling contest showcases the delightful and lively atmosphere we have come to associate with African religious sentiments.[78]

---

fear of his power. His priestess stood by the sacred fire which she built in the heart of the cave and proclaimed the will of the god. The fire did not burn with a flame. The glowing logs only served to light up vaguely the dark figure of the priestess." Achebe, *Things Fall Apart*, 16–17.

[78] "The drums were still beating, persistent and unchanging. Their sound was no longer a separate thing from the living village. It was like the pulsation of its heart. It throbbed in the air, in the sunshine, and even in the trees, and filled the village with excitement.... There were seven drums and they were arranged according to their sizes in a long wooden

Thus, rhythm, excitement, and frenzy, those supposed iconic marks of African religious expressions, are in fact "the unmistakable wrestling dance—quick, light and gay,"[79] or the overriding sentiments of other social functions that are only tangentially related to the traditional religion rather than typifying it. Interpreting Achebe in *Things Fall Apart*, one readily comes to the conclusion that while Africans may be extravagant in their joy when at play, they have the tendency, or rather intuition, of assuming a more or less severe and somber air when they pray. Africans understand that prayer is not, and should not be, a joke. Furthermore, Achebe contrasted the gravity of the pre-colonial Igbo people in religious matters with the jovial mood of evangelical Protestantism as follows: "Then the missionaries burst into song. It was one of those gay and rollicking tunes of evangelism which had the power of plucking at silent and dusty chords in the heart of an I[g]bo man."[80]

Protestantism is an attempt to demystify and popularize the Catholic Faith. It is the removal of elements which offend contemporary sensibility,

---

basket. Three men beat them with sticks, working feverishly from one drum to another. They were possessed by the spirit of the drums. . . . Old men nodded to the beat of the drums and remembered the days when they wrestled to its intoxicating rhythm." Achebe, *Things Fall Apart*, 44, 46, 47.

[79] Achebe, 42.

[80] Achebe, 146.

and the injection of accessible and "respectable" notions. Such popularization amounts to secularization, the turning away from the divine to the human. This is why the Protestantization of Europe was only one step away from its secularization. Similarly, the identification of native African cultus with secular African cultures in the popular psyche, the identification of how indigenous Africans pray with how they play, and the transfer of this playful ethos (rather than the prayerful) into Catholic liturgy as inculturation constitute genuine liturgical popularization and secularization. It is the direct parallel of introducing rock music or operatic singing into the liturgy in the United States or in Italy in the name of inculturation. Such actions merely trivialize and secularize the liturgy, stripping it of its mystery and solemnity.

The world-acclaimed *Missa Luba*, "an African setting of the Mass sung in Latin,"[81] originally performed by a Congolese choir under the direction and inspiration of Belgian priest Guido Haazen, was developed entirely from tunes drawn from the Congolese repertoire of traditional folk music rather than from the stock of religious music. Why? Maybe this is because the religious music is largely unpopular or largely undeveloped. These two possibilities are derivatives, I think,

---

[81] Doris Anna McDaniel, "Analysis of the Missa Luba," Master's Thesis, University of Rochester (1973), ii.

of the extreme austerity of the native African
religious disposition. We do not thereby "incul-
turate the Mass in the Congo" when we ask
the Congolese to pray as they would play. We
merely trivialize and secularize the sacred function.[82] *Missa Luba* was a huge success in several
concert halls in Europe and across the world,
and rightly so, because it was an innovative
composition for concerts, a novel exhibition of
a rich African secular music tradition. It was not
intended, nor was it suitable, for use as prayer at
Mass, just as operatic settings of the Mass are
unsuitable in Italy or in any part of the Catholic
world. This thought was more fully developed in
St. Pius X's *Tra Le Sollecitudini*, which declared:

> Among the different kinds of modern music, that
> which appears less suitable for accompanying
> the functions of public worship is the theatrical
> style, which was in the greatest vogue, especially
> in Italy, during the last century. This of its very
> nature is diametrically opposed to Gregorian
> Chant and classic polyphony, and therefore to the
> most important law of all good sacred music.[83]

To maintain the effective and necessary demar-
cation between the playground and the sacred
ground, St. Pius X insisted that musical compositions "which are admitted in the Church may

---

[82] [See chapter 9 below.—*Ed.*]

[83] Pius X, *Tra Le Sollecitudini*, 1903.

contain nothing profane, be free from reminis-
cences of motifs adopted in the theaters, and be
not fashioned even in their external forms after
the manner of profane pieces."[84]

There is hardly any doubt that *Missa Luba* and
other African musical compositions of the Mass
contributed to the development of the Zaire
Usage.[85] Today, whether in a Mass celebrated
according to the Zaire Usage or in any other
inculturated forms of the Roman Rite celebrated
in Africa, music in the *Missa Luba* style, or forms
much more unrestrained and theatrical, have
become normative. While it is true that in some
instances such inculturated liturgical services do
afford some opportunity for prayer and union
with the Sacrifice, I have had many experiences
in several parishes across Nigeria in which the
sacred function was reduced almost to a mere
jamboree, especially during fundraisers such as
Uka bia nara Ngozi, Harvest Thanksgiving or
Seed Sowing, etc. Unfortunately, such fundraisers
within the Mass are increasing in frequency and
excesses in many parts of Nigeria.

The disturbing secularization of the liturgy that
goes with inculturation bridges the gap Achebe

---

[84] Ibid. For a detailed commentary on this document, see
Patrick Brill, *The Great Sacred Music Reform of Pope St. Pius
X: The Genesis, Interpretation, and Implementation of the Motu
Proprio "Tra le Sollecitudini"* (Lincoln, NE: Os Justi Press, 2025).
[85] Chase, "History and Analysis."

noted in *Things Fall Apart* between a stern native African approach to religion and the happy-clappy mood of Protestantism, especially the Pentecostal camp. It should be noted that the popularization introduced into the Mass under the guise of inculturation is often behind the latest trends in Pentecostalism, whose raison d'être is religious secularization or rapprochement with the Zeitgeist. One result of this state of things is that Catholics unsatisfied with half-measure popularization in their parishes stream into one of the up-to-date Protestant congregations. Hence, inculturation is arguably the main reason why Catholics in Nigeria defect to Pentecostal or Evangelical groups.

Besides the "invocation of ancestors" and lively singing and dancing, other unique features of the Zaire Usage that have been held up as genuinely African include the role of a liturgical announcer, which parallels the role of a town crier in many African communities, and the placement and nature of the penitential rite, "whose structure is inspired by the African palaver."[86] The last two innovations are drawn from the social organization and operation of African communities. There is no doubt that the Church's liturgy and organization have been influenced and have influenced the structure of secular government over

---

[86] Conference Episcopale du Zaire, quoted by Chase, 33.

the course of history.[87] However, the services of town criers were certainly not restricted to African communities, nor were they ever employed in Africa or anywhere else for the moderation of the religious function of the community in the capacity of the "liaison between the priest and the assembly"[88] as stipulated in the Zaire Usage. In traditional African religions, as in many other religions of the world, past and present, the priest or priestess is the liaison between the people and the deity. An "official" role for the town crier or "announcer or herald, who is neither a religious nor a priest"[89] beyond the marketplace or street corners and well within the shrine of the gods, is unheard of, and cannot even be imagined.

Touching the placement and nature of the penitential rite that was said to have been inspired by the African palaver, it is obvious that parleying and reconciliation need not belong exclusively to Africans. Neither should the liturgy be tinkered with in order to teach history lessons or re-enact social practices long obsolete.[90] Overall, it is hard

---

[87] Josef A. Jungmann, *The Mass of the Roman Rite: Its Origins and Development* (Westminster, MD: Christian Classics, 1986), vol. 1, pp. 68–69; Marshall W. Baldwin, *The Mediaeval Church* (New York: Cornell University Press, 1953), 60; Wielzen, "Popular Religiosity and Roman Liturgy," 198–99.

[88] Chase, "History and Analysis," 32.

[89] Ibid.

[90] Nche, Okwuosa, Nwaoga, "Revisiting the Concept of Inculturation."

to see anything genuinely African and at the same time genuinely relevant to the liturgy in the two organizational innovations in the Zaire Usage, but it is not hard to see a common thread in the novelties: the weakening of the ministerial priesthood in favor of lay participation. The "announcer" innovation does this overtly while the allusion to the African palaver in positioning the penitential rite approaches the same goal more covertly.

The failure of inculturation and insights from this failure

If inculturation or liturgical adaptation seeks to help the local population pray in a way which, while being natural to them, has been purified and elevated by the light of the Gospel and the Christian civilization, then inculturation, as has been practiced in Africa with the Zaire Usage at its apex, has been an unqualified failure. This same conclusion applies to inculturation implemented in other parts of the Catholic world. The relevant data cited earlier show that no modern effort at liturgical inculturation has invigorated the local Catholic population or accelerated the conversion of non-Catholics. On the contrary, in every part of the world, various sects and false religions are snatching souls at alarming rates from the fold of Christ.

One thing that must be clear from the failure of the recent efforts at inculturation across the Catholic world is that true inculturation, like any genuine cultural advancement, knows of no central committee of experts and elites working out an on-the-spot program of revision or innovation. A genuine culture grows organically. It borrows; it always does; but only that which has grown organically and stood the test of time. It survives and flourishes by establishing clear demarcations between the various aspects or levels of life in the community, without disconnecting these. The demarcations erected by genuine cultures are "semi-permeable," i.e., they allow the exchange of refined elements between the cultural levels. In a balanced culture, each level grows naturally, influencing and being influenced by the other levels, but in such a way that the cultus, theology, and/or ultimate philosophy of the people have the final and binding say in what is uprooted or allowed to grow.

The example of antebellum Irish American society
The musical organization of Irish Catholic parish life in pre-war United States provides us a good example of a natural ordering of community life, showcasing organic development, natural demarcations, and the flux of refined elements between the cultural segments over

time. The five distinct musical categories that existed in this community—evidence of natural demarcations—may be described as liturgical, devotional, sodality, social, and home music.[91]

Liturgical music, which is usually in Latin and following the norms of the universal Church, is at the heart of the community and used exclusively in solemn liturgical ceremonies. Next is devotional music, which could be in the vernacular, but in style and text suitable for religious use. Devotional music may feature in "low" Masses or other liturgical or extra-liturgical ceremonies. The sodality music category included not only the music used in pious associations in the parish, but also the music produced by political clubs, parochial schools, and other interest groups that meet or are organized under the auspices of the parish. The music in this category is usually in the vernacular and may vary substantially in style and subject. The various forms of music employed in Catholic public events such as St Patrick's Day celebrations and other cultural events are here described as social music. Social music is typically in the vernacular and the style is dictated by popular taste. At their homes, Catholics made music for purposes of devotion,

---

[91] Robert R. Grimes, *How Shall We Sing in a Foreign Land?* (Notre Dame, IN: University of Notre Dame Press, 1996), 8–10.

amusement, and education, which may be in the vernacular or in Latin.

It should be noted that the category of devotional music is a hybrid of sacred and secular music with elements of the former predominating. The secular elements may predominate in the sodality music, which is also a hybrid category. These hybridizations are evidences of the natural exchange occurring across the musical demarcations. The overall musical organization was profoundly successful in inculcating and transmitting the Catholic Faith and the Irish traditional culture—as much of that culture that could be re-lived in a foreign land. The community joyfully and profitably "sang the 'music of the Catholic Church' and the songs of Thomas Moore, Samuel Lover, and the 'national airs of Ireland'"[92] in Latin, Irish, and English. Both sacred and secular music performed by the Irish Catholic community attained professional excellence and attracted huge crowds of people, Catholics and non-Catholics, when performed at Mass or concert.[93] There was no incentivization of bad music by forcing it on helpless parishioners under the guise of liturgical adaptation.[94] Naturally, but

---

[92] Grimes, 8–10, 57.
[93] Grimes, 61–66, 109–11.
[94] However, without the benefit of the twentieth century reform of St. Pius X, it was not surprising that some

not without some controversies, cross-pollination between music categories abounded, with the local hierarchy of the Catholic Church serving as the ultimate arbiter in sacred matters and popular taste the arbiter in the secular.[95]

The Irish Catholic music life in pre-war United States clearly shows that to engage the cultural depth of a local population, there is no need to replace Latin with Gaeilge or Igbo or to substitute Catholic pieties with druidic or animist rituals. Even before the migration to America, and this for centuries and in the face of the most brutal persecution, Ireland held fast with love to the truth and liturgy of the Catholic Church expressed mostly in Latin. This language and discipline that was described as "dead" and "foreign" was certainly alive and familiar to the Irish soul. So great was Ireland's loyalty to the Traditional Latin Mass that men and women, literate or unlettered, were willing to, and many in fact did, give up everything—land, culture, and life—for the joy of "Introibo ad altare Dei."[96] Shockingly, such an undaunted Catholic will as was seen

---

performances may have been "too entertaining" for Mass (Grimes, 61). Overall, there was great concern to preserve the integrity of the Mass as well as to advance the Irish cultural experiences of the people.

[95] Grimes, 32, 55, 112–14, 134–35.

[96] Augustine Hayden, O. M. Cap., *Ireland's Loyalty to the Mass* (Manchester, NH: Sophia Institute Press, 2023).

among the Irish who "survived dungeon, fire, and sword"[97] did not survive liturgical inculturation and disciplinary accommodation to contemporary cultures.[98] It follows, then, that while inculturation is made to pass as an innocuous and beneficial practice, the overwhelming evidence shows that it is a life-threatening invasive procedure with no known case of holistic success.

◇◇◇◇◇

The inescapable conclusion from our brief survey is that whether in Ireland, Nigeria, Brazil, the Philippines, the USA, or any part of the Catholic world, modern inculturation was a wrong turn for the Church and for civilization. "And if you have taken a wrong turning," C. S. Lewis remarked, "then to go forward does not get you any nearer [to your goal]."[99] This is common sense. "If you are on the wrong road, progress means doing an about-turn and walking back to the right road…"[100] What we must do cannot be simpler and more concrete. And we know what the right road to walk back to is. In Microsoft Windows, it used to be called the "Last Known

---

[97] Twomey, *The End of Irish Catholicism?*, 34.
[98] Twomey, 35–36.
[99] C. S. Lewis, *Mere Christianity* (New York: Macmillan Publishing Company, 1952), 36.
[100] Lewis, 36.

Good Configuration" option. In the Catholic Church, that configuration has always been the Traditional Latin Mass and its associated liturgical disciplines. The least any bishop can do is to give the Traditional Latin Mass a chance. Let us start there generously and see the dry bones rise again![101]

ADDENDA

The following note was sent to the editor of this book as it was in preparation.

AS A CATHOLIC IN UGANDA, I WISH to share three points with you that, I believe, emphasize the respect all honest Catholics should pay to our pre-conciliar Catholic inheritance.

Firstly, Fr Christophe Nouveau, IBP, the pastor of our TLM Community in Kampala, wrote a Master's thesis on the role of the traditional liturgy in the evangelisation of Uganda over a ninety-year period, that is, from 1879, the year in which the Missionaries of Africa (aka White Fathers) arrived in Uganda, to 1969, when Pope Paul VI made the first-ever historic apostolic pilgrimage to Africa, to honour the Ugandan Martyrs, whom he had canonised in 1964. Fr Christophe's work was published in 2022 as *The*

---

[101] Cf. Ezekiel 37:1–10.

Role of the Traditional Latin Mass in the Evangelisation of the Catholic Church in Uganda (1879-1969) from Blessed Hope Publishing.

Secondly, the address given by Pope Paul VI on 1 August 1969 to members of the Catholic Church at the Metropolitan Cathedral in Kampala is illuminating,[102] especially when one recalls that this was about four months before the Apostolic Constitution, *Missale Romanum*, issued in April of that year, was to take effect throughout the Latin Church. It should be emphasized that the papal praise of the remarkable growth of the Church in Uganda, not only quantitatively, but more importantly, qualitatively, is obviously referring to a *pre-conciliar ecclesial reality* in Uganda, before the imposition of inculturation by the Western liturgists of the post-Vatican II period.

Thirdly, to mark the centenary of the Catholic Faith in Uganda in 1979, a book was written by Fr Yves Tourigny (another "White Father"), the Kampala archdiocesan archivist at the time.[103] The title of Fr Tourigny's work is taken from the papal address highlighted above. It is remarkable to note, however, that despite the book's copious

---

[102] For the address, see www.vatican.va/content/paul-vi/en/speeches/1969/august/documents/hf_p-vi_spe_19690801_chiesa-cattolica.html.

[103] See Yves Tourigny, *So Abundant a Harvest: The Catholic Church in Uganda 1879–1979* (London: Darton, Longman and Todd, 1979).

details about the history of the Catholic Church
in Uganda, the formative and inspiring role of
the traditional Latin liturgy is not addressed! An
unsuspecting reader might assume a liturgical
continuum throughout the one hundred years.
This kind of sloppy treatment constitutes a critical
lapse in historical memory, a denial of the spiritual treasures of our pre-conciliar Catholic past,
and, in effect, a falsification, deliberate or inadver-
tent, of Catholic truth. This is why Fr Nouveau's
work is such an important step in rehabilitating
our Catholic heritage in Uganda.

*Fr. Nouveau himself, when he read the manu-
script of the present book, reacted in these words:*

AS A PRIEST CELEBRATING THE TRA-
ditional Latin Mass in East Africa for twenty years,
I appreciate your collective work *Is African Catholicism a "Vatican II Success Story"?* For the story is
not one of success; the Catholic Faith has been
damaged by the new spirit of this council in
Africa like everywhere else, even if the consequences are not of the same magnitude (yet).

When Vatican II took place, the work of
evangelisation was still going on; the missionary congregations had been on the continent for
sixty to eighty years, which is short in terms of
Church history. So the dynamic of evangelisation

that entered well before the Council continued, in my view, for around thirty years afterwards, before the negative effects clearly appeared. It is from the end of the 90s that we see a decrease in the percentage of Catholics in most African countries, as well as the appearance of new religious groups such as Pentecostals and evangelicals which increase by recruiting the Catholic faithful.

Before, the traditional Latin Mass that started the process of evangelisation of Africa protected the faith of the Catholics; its absence means they are vulnerable. Now there is a race between Catholic priests and Protestant pastors to attract people, especially the youth, by ceremonies with dancing, music, and miracles. Catholics have lost the meaning of the sacrifice of the Mass.

In Africa, the number of faithful increases due to a high birthrate. In Uganda, during the ten years I have been here, the population has increased by 11.3 million! So the fact that the population of Catholics during this decade has increased by 3.5 million is not surprising and cannot be attributed to Vatican II. There are more worrisome numbers we should pay attention to: Catholics were 39.3% of the population in 2014 and now they are 37%, with Pentecostals and Evangelicals increasing from 10.9 to 14.3%.

Seminaries are full and Africa even exports priests to Western countries. But here the priesthood is too often a form of social promotion. On September 29, 2006, Benedict XVI in his ad limina adress to the Bishops of Malawi stated: "Help your clergy not to fall into the trap of seeing the priesthood as a means of social advancement . . ." When a priest is ordained here, the parishioners buy him a car—whereas those leaving university as medical doctors, engineers, or lawyers will need several years before they can buy a car for themselves.

There are nevertheless signs of hope. With the internet, Catholics youths in Africa easily find out what the Catholic Church was before Vatican II. Such youths organise invitations to priests to visit them and bring the traditional Latin Mass. We also find in the seminaries of traditionalist communities vocations from Africa. The hierarchy of the Church in Africa also recognizes some of the consequences of Vatican II. In Kampala, the Archbishop Cyprian Lwanga on February 1, 2020 issued a law: "It is fitting to return to the more reverent method of receiving the Eucharist on the tongue."

8

INCULTURATION THROUGH TRADITION

CLAUDIO SALVUCCI

O NE SOMETIMES MEETS WITH the notion that "traditional Catholi- cism", as understood today, is wholly unsuited to the non-European mind. One prom- inent professor and musician has even boldly stated that:

> pastors must take care to introduce current liturgical reforms in a manner conducive to the cultural expression of worshiping communities as mandated by Vatican II. African American cultur- ally based worship models are forward looking, progressive, creative and universal in nature and will never fit into a pre-Vatican II mold.[1]

In this thinking, Vatican II represents a kind of cultural zero point. The Novus Ordo Missae is granted a lofty status as a de-Romanized, de- Europeanized, culturally "neutral" Catholicism— as the only truly primeval base from which true authentic inculturation can then properly begin.

---

[1] *Uncommon Faithfulness: The Black Catholic Experience,* ed. M. Shawn Copeland (Maryknoll, NY: Orbis Books, 2009), accessed online at Google books, no page.

The sentiment is very typical of the last half century: that the classical Roman Missal has little or nothing to contribute to the liturgical and devotional life of modern Catholics. That attitude is not restricted to liturgical inculturation proponents, of course, but among them it seems particularly pronounced. Whether that thesis is historically defensible we'll come to in a minute.

But first, it's important to point out that such a total repudiation of tradition is a Faustian bargain: its promise of a glorious, liberated future subtly hides a ruthless eradication of the past. It tempts us with immense wealth we can bestow on our grandchildren, if only we agree to forge them from the melted-down remnants of our grandparents' heirlooms. The etymological connection between "culture" and "cultivation" is not accidental—and every gardener knows that the difference between pruning limbs and sawing into the trunk is the difference between life and death.

There is a plain fact about the Novus Ordo Missae that we must finally acknowledge. And that is that the radical break in 1970 was not solely a single rupture with a wider, general patrimony of the Western Church. It was also a thousand ruptures with local, national, and cultural patrimonies—many of them non-European and hundreds of years old. In my book *The Roman Rite in the Algonquian and Iroquoian Missions* (2008),

I discussed how just such a break played out in the Indian Missions of Eastern Canada and the U. S. In the 1940s, priests who visited the town of Kahnawake, the site of St. Kateri's shrine, marveled at the sheer wealth of local liturgical tradition they found there—including plainchant and polyphony in the Mohawk language. This tradition was broken with the introduction of the English Mass at Kahnawake—and there and elsewhere, many American Indians felt betrayed by the loss of what they themselves called, tellingly, "the Indian Mass."

Whatever we want to argue about the Novus Ordo Missae, there is one thing we can never say about it: that it was the Mass of our ancestors. And that is universally true no matter who our ancestors were. St. Kateri and the Kahnawakeronnon who hunted in the forests of Quebec did not know it. The Servant of God Augustus Tolton and other former slaves who battled racial prejudice did not know it. The English recusants who sailed to Maryland on the Ark and the Dove did not know it. My great-grandparents who labored under the Italian sun did not know it. No one anywhere in the world knew it.

This is not a mere rhetorical point; it is a glaring unacknowledged contradiction at the heart of our liturgical life. How can we assert the inviolate nature of non-Catholic customs and demand their preservation in the Church, while simultaneously discarding our native Catholic customs and culture in the process? A case has been made by Monsignor Pope for gospel music in predominately black churches, and no doubt many self-declared progressives would heartily agree with his arguments.[2] But Monsignor also offers his parishioners the Traditional Latin Mass.[3] After all, it would hardly make sense to promote the music of black Protestantism as the ne plus ultra of black religious culture while rejecting the liturgy and music that defined black Catholicism for centuries. Inculturation may make use of cultural norms that are Protestant in origin (Advent wreaths and the Ordinariates are good examples). But it must give priority to that culture's Catholic heritage wherever it can, or it is intrinsically self-defeating.

Bishop Joseph Perry of Chicago is among those successfully realizing this principle. His Excellency is a notable proponent of the traditional Roman Mass. He has also served as chairman of the USCCB committee on African American Catholics, vice-president of the National Black Catholic Congress, and postulator

---

[2] See Msgr. Charles Pope, "What is Sacred Music? Historically it's a bit more complex than you may think," *Community in Mission*, December 9, 2013.

[3] Or *did*, prior to Cardinal Wilton Gregory's cancellation of it in the wake of *Traditionis Custodes*.

for the sainthood cause of Father Tolton. In a discussion of inculturation, he argued:

> It occurs to me that what is black and Catholic is not wholly the same as what is black and Protestant. Although black Christians hold membership in greatest numbers in the Protestant traditions and have fine-tuned a black Protestant style, what is black and Catholic carries its own genius. We must explore what is uniquely ours and enrich it. We must steer clear of adapting wholesale Protestant modes in order to impress African Americans with our brand of religion.[4]

Putting those ideas into practice, Bishop Perry offered a Solemn High Pontifical Mass last year in honor of Father Tolton[5] that featured motets by Afro-Brazilian composer José Maurício Nunes Garcia.[6] It would be hard to argue that this Mass failed the standards of inculturation. The traditional Mass all by itself provided an essential liturgical connection to Father Tolton—it being the only Mass he ever knew or offered. And by linking Tolton to Nunes Garcia's sacred music, the Mass was

---

[4] Joseph Perry, "Black Catholic Worship: Some Reflections," *American Catholic Press*, www.americancatholicpress.org/ Bishop_%20Perry_Black_Catholic_Worship.html.

[5] On YouTube under the title "Tolton Mass April 25, 2016," www.youtube.com/watch?v=wYRBoeNomE8.

[6] See the biography at https://chevalierdesaintgeorges.home-stead.com/nunes.html.

implicitly creating a distinct African tradition within the classical Roman liturgy.

I'd like to pause on that verb "creating" for a bit.

Can we not see from His Excellency's good example that there is no loss of cultural creativity and progress in promoting the traditional Mass? There is no room to talk of fossilization, of stagnation, of repressively stifling traditionalism in an environment where black Catholics delve ever deeper into their own pre-Vatican II historical material, discover lost treasures mostly forgotten by other liturgists and scholars, and reintroduce them to new generations. I do not know whether "good Father Gus" ever had the time or resources to deliberately bring composers like Nunes Garcia into the schola of St. Monica's. But with the resources we have, we can now do that. And so much more besides.

No matter what our ethnicity, the Church's long, long tradition is like a treasure trove in the attic, most of which has just been collecting dust and is ever in need of enterprising scholars to sift through, analyze, and bring into the present.

Old St. Joseph's church in Philadelphia had a community of black parishioners since the late 1700s—the French diplomat François Rene de Chateaubriand wrote a hymn specially for them that was then translated into English and was

regularly sung into the turn of the century.[7] A
special Sunday Mass was offered for black Catholics,[8] as well a Sunday Vespers service known
as "Evening Hymn". The band of celebrated
black composer Francis Johnson (1792–1844)
and the black vocalist Elizabeth Taylor Greenfield
(1809?–1876)[9] were featured, attracting crowds
of all colors with music that was "sweet and
silvery beyond description."[10] And that all from
one single black Catholic community! Most of
the great orders and organizations that form the
pillars of black Catholicism today—the Black
Catholic Congresses, the Society of St. Joseph,
the Oblate Sisters of Providence, the Knights
of St. Peter Claver—arose in the pre-Vatican
II period, and their archives no doubt contain
many, many more fruitful avenues for research.

Even secular scholars of the African diaspora are providing us with some fascinating

---

[7] See "Chateaubriand in Philadelphia 1791—Composes a
Hymn for the Colored Catholics," in *The American Catholic
Historical Researches for 1899* (Philadelphia: Martin I. J. Griffin,
1899), 151. (May be found at Google Books by searching
"hail happy queen chateaubriand.")

[8] See Martin I. J. Griffin, *History of "Old St. Joseph's" Philadelphia* (Philadelphia: I. C. B. U. Journal Print, 1882), 12.

[9] www.blackpast.org/african-american-history/greenfield-eliz-
abeth-taylor-1819-1876/.

[10] Eleanor C. Donnelly, *A Memoir of Father Felix Joseph Barbelin, S. J.* (New York: Christian Press Association Publishing
Company, 1886), 203.

information that can prove immensely valuable
to the goal of inculturation. The Kongo Kingdom, once assumed to be only superficially converted by the Portuguese, is now increasingly
seen as a self-defining Catholic nation where
the faith had a profound impact on its folklore
and culture.[11] A fifth to a quarter of the Africans
brought to America as slaves came from this
region, of whom many were likely baptized Catholics. In much of the southern U.S. they were
mostly subsumed into Protestant denominations,
though some rebelled.[12] When brought to Catholic nations, on the other hand, they quickly
organized confraternities under saints such as
St. Benedict the Moor. Processions in his honor
were performed "with such devotion, majesty
and pomp" that in 1619 they were attended by
the King of Spain.[13] In French Louisiana, the
"Mardi Gras Indians," often dismissed as a some-
what tawdry imitation of Indians or Wild West
shows, have been connected by recent studies

[11] See John Thornton, "The Development of an African
Catholic Church in the Kingdom of Kongo, 1491–1750,"
The Journal of African History, vol. 25, no. 2 (1984): 147–67.
[12] See Matthew J. Cressler, "African Catholics and Slave Rebel-
lion in Early American History," *Religion in American History*,
January 31, 2014, https://usreligion.blogspot.com/2014/01/
african-catholics-and-slave-rebellion.html.
[13] See Margaret Cormack, ed., *Saints and Their Cults in the
Atlantic World* (Columbia, SC: University of South Carolina
Press, 2007), 30.

to Afro-Iberian Catholic ceremonies throughout the diaspora.[14]

We should also remember the degree to which, from the very beginning, black Catholics consciously repatriated the heritage of Roman Africa, already present within the Latin Church but long since uprooted by the Islamic invasion. By repeatedly naming churches after St. Augustine, St. Monica, and St. Cyprian, black churches were not merely selecting heavenly patrons. They were also locally modifying the Roman liturgical calendar in an African direction, because the patronal feast of a parish church was automatically raised to the highest rank and given an octave for all the clergy attached to it. (Here perhaps we realize what damage was done with the 1955 decimation of liturgical octaves!)

Moreover, we have already seen how St. Benedict the Moor's feast was kept with great festivity by members of the African diaspora. But this feast is not found in the general Roman or American calendars either pre- or post-Vatican II; it is a peculiarity of their own tradition, long shared only with local calendars in the Franciscan order and Sicily, and now spread to African nations like Ghana, Kenya, and Nigeria. There is

---

[14] See Jeroen Dewulf, *From the Kingdom of Kongo to the Congo Square: Kongo Dances and the Origins of the Mardi Gras Indians* (Lafayette: University of Louisiana at Lafayette Press, 2017).

certainly ample opportunity for more additions along these same lines, as the Roman Martyrology lists dozens of African saints who are not found in the general calendar.

If we wish to make use of all this history, the way forward should now be clear. Creative inculturation ought to come not at the expense of tradition, but *through* tradition. It must continue to build on any new information that comes to light and revive old practices that have been allowed to lapse, while respecting the integral character of the rituals already used, expected, and cherished by the people over generations.

Cutting ourselves off from traditional Catholicism does not keep us from being contaminated by excessive European influence. It just keeps us from discovering the fascinating ways over the centuries that non-European communities and cultures interacted with the Faith, enriched it, and made it their own.

9

ZAIREAN—OR SARUM?
THE FORGOTTEN
CONGOLESE LITURGY

CLAUDIO SALVUCCI

THE ZAIREAN USE OCCASION-
ally comes up in the news,[1] but despite
an interest in the Catholic Congo,[2] I'm
afraid I know too little about it to comment
intelligently. Little profit can come from a polem-
icism—on either side—that insists on promoting
or critiquing various attempts at inculturation
without spending a great deal of time studying
the culture in question. Culture is, after all, at the
heart of the issue—and cultures differ.

For this very reason, even someone well-
situated to discuss North American Indian
inculturation along the St. Lawrence[3] ought to
keep a respectful distance when the Indians in

---

[1] See, e.g., Courtney Mares, "Pope Francis celebrates Mass
in the Congolese rite: 'Peace begins with us,'" *Catholic News
Agency*, July 3, 2022.

[2] See my article "Images of the Catholic Congo," *Liturgical
Arts Journal*, November 23, 2017.

[3] I refer to my detailed study *The Roman Rite in the Algonquian
and Iroquoian Missions from the Colonial Period to the Second
Vatican Council* (Merchantville, NJ: Evolution Publishing, 2008).

question live along the Amazon.[4] However we can nonetheless stress an important universal that has been sadly absent from much of the discussion over the last fifty years. Inculturation, we are told, must respect local *tradition*. And that is true. But too often, only pagan or secular tradition is meant, and that is where the fatal error creeps in. What inculturation actually must respect most of all is a culture's own *Catholic tradition.*

We need to go back in history, as far back as we can, to the first meeting between the faith and the culture. And then we trace how both faith and culture entwined through the centuries, creating a local Church that was the natural fusion of that process. And this applies as much to American Indians or Congolese as it does to Europeans and European-Americans.

It is a titanic error of judgment to assume that no cultural fusion worth mentioning happened before Vatican II. And that is manifestly the case in the region served by the Zairean Use.

The Kingdom of Kongo, founded in 1390, was first visited by Portuguese missionaries during the reign of King João I in 1491. Under his son, the pious Afonso I, Catholicism became the state

---

[4] See my article "The Amazon Synod, and the Liberal Enemies of Inculturation," October 10, 2019, https://hoquessing.com/the-amazon-synod-and-the-liberal-enemies-of-inculturation/.

ALVARO VI OF KONGO (1581–1641)

religion, after which Kongo was duly recognized as a Catholic Kingdom by the Pope and the crowns of Europe. A Papal Bull of Pope Urban VIII even authorized the Capuchin missionaries to crown the Kings of Kongo according to the Catholic Rite of Coronation.

Anyone who uncritically transplants jaded European modernism into the minds of the indigenous Congolese might be surprised by that last fact. But historical accounts indicate that subsaharan Africans did not scorn the pomp and ceremony of the Baroque European liturgy—to the contrary, they seem to have been quite eager participants in it.

The Italian chronicler Filippo Pigafetta noted in 1591 that the Cathedral of the Holy Cross in M'Banza Kongo had attached to it "about twenty-eight canons, various chaplains, a chapel master, and choristers, besides being provided with an organ, bells, and everything else necessary for Divine service."

Missionary Girolamo Merolla (1650–1697) informs us that there were eighteen churches in the dominions of the Count of Sogno. On the feast of St. James, every governor of a city was obliged on pain of deposition and a fine to either attend or send a representative to the Banza of Sogno to assist at the first Mass. A throne was set up for the Count in the marketplace. Dressed majestically in an embroidered scarlet cloak, a coral rope, a crown of feathers, and a cross of gold around his neck, the Count received a benediction from the missionaries and then demonstrated his skill with a bow and arrow as well as with a musket. Military exercises then took place under his watch, and symbolic tributes were brought forth from the various areas of his dominion. "This Ceremony is begun on St.

RUINS OF THE CATHEDRAL IN M'BANZA KONGO
(PHOTO: MADJEY FERNANDES)

James's day, by reason that Apostle is look'd upon as the Patron and Protector of all these Parts, and that for having given a famous Victory to the King of Congo against the idolaters on his day." Great crowds from the surrounding areas came to partake of the festivities.

Some fascinating details are given about the Count of Sogno's liturgical roles during the various parts of the Mass:

> While Mass is saying, at the reading of the Gospel he has a lighted Torch presented to him, which having religiously receiv'd, he gives to one of his Pages to hold till the Consummation be over, and when the Gospel is done he has the Mass-Book given him to kiss. On festival Days he is twice incens'd with the Censor, and at the end of Mass he is to go to the Altar

to receive Benediction from the Priest, who laying his Hands upon his Head while he is kneeling, pronounces some pious and devout Ejaculations.

Even long afterward, when the kingdom was in its decline, an expedition to San Salvador in 1879 noted that "Old crucifixes are to be found amongst the insignia of some chiefs; and now and then a Portuguese missal." Around the same time, "missals and other books" were mentioned

PEDRO V, KING OF KONGO; REIGNED 1859–1891

omnibus conspicua: *Eminium*, nostro ævo *Agatham* appellamus, *Lamecum* prope Durium, ac *Viseum.*

Ultra Durium extra Lusitaniæ fines in provincia veteri Tarraconensi *Bracara* Gallæciæ Metropolis, *Portugale*, *Dumium* prope Bracaram, quod dicebatur Monasterium Familiæ regiæ ; *Britonia* prope *Vianam* , quæ dicitur *de Caminha.* Temporum vicissitudine transeunte, novæ Metropoles, novi Episcopatus erecti sunt, veteresque alii extincti. Emerita Episcopali honore non fruitur, Olysipo , & Ebora Metropolitica sublimantur dignitate : Ossonobæ cathedra ad Silvensem Urbem , indeque ad Pharensem , ubi remanet, translata est. Pax Julia Cathedralem Ecclesiam non retinet : in Transtagana provincia novæ institutæ sunt Cathedræ , Elvensis, ac Portalegrensis. In Extrematura novus extat Collipodensis Episcopatus, quem sermo patrius *Leiriensem* appellat. In Beirensi provincia desiit Eminiensis. Ultra Durium Dumium , ac Britonia sine Sede, & Episcopo vetus nomen vix habent : & intra Bracarensis Ecclesiæ limites apud Mirandam in transmontana provincia recens floret Episcoporum Sedes.

Nec tantum in Portugaliæ continenti novæ Metropoles, novique sunt Episcopatus ; verum & ultra mare, quâ longe, lateque Lusitani adierunt Lusitanæ ditioni novas possessiones adquisitum: qui cum Lusitanæ Ecclesiæ eosdem ritus, ac eandem servent disciplinam, ipsorumque alii Olysiponensi Metropoli pareant, non est cur silentio indigno prætermittantur. *Ceptensis* in Africa ; ast jam Antistite caret; *Funchalensis*, & *Angrensis* in insulis maris Oceani, *Promontorii viridis* , *Congensis*, seu *Angolensis* , *S. Thomæ*, *Goanensis apud Indos*, *Cochinensis*, *Malacanensis*, *Machaonensis*, *Angamalensis*, *de Meliapor*, *de Pekim* , & *Nankim* apud Sinas: in America, Episcopatus *S. Salvatoris Bahiensis* omnium Sanctorum, *S. Sebastiani Fluminis Januarii*, *Olindæ* , *de Maragnano* , *de Pará*, *S. Pauli*, *S. Mariæ de Monte Carmelo*, quibus duæ Prælaturæ exemptæ fuerunt additæ.

A HISTORY OF THE CHURCH IN PORTUGAL (1759), LISTING THE CONGO/ANGOLA (*CONGENSIS SEU ANGOLENSIS*) SUFFRAGAN TO LISBON (*OLYSIPONENSIS*)

among old church furnishings of the Portuguese missionaries that were still treasured at San Salvador "and the natives would not part with them on any account."

These fascinating tidbits of information give a tantalizing glimpse into how the medieval Roman liturgy was embraced by the Congolese court and its subjects.

They also raise an important and perhaps uncomfortable question.

How much of what passes for authentic Congolese inculturation nowadays is actually just a modern primitivist's stereotype of what Congolese liturgy *ought* to look like, rather than reflecting how the historical Congolese liturgy actually *did* look like for all of its long history?

We don't, unfortunately, have a completely clear picture of the ancient Congolese liturgy—perhaps if any of those old Portuguese Missals are still around, they might shed light upon the question.

We know that the Congolese church was suffragan to the See of Lisbon. But not even Lisbon's liturgy in this time period is known for certain. Once the city was recaptured from the Moors in 1147, the Sarum Rite was established there by its first bishop: the English monk Gilbert of Hastings. Through the centuries, the Sarum Rite seems to have gradually declined until 1536, when Lisbon officially switched to the Roman

Rite. But it's unclear how that switch happened, and where the last holdouts were.

So, in the 1490s and soon afterward—well before the Council of Trent and at the tail end of the medieval era—could the first missionaries sent out from Lisbon and their successors have been celebrating the Sarum Rite, or perhaps a Sarum-influenced Roman Rite? Could Afonso's son Henrique Kinu a Mvemba, who became a priest and then was consecrated a bishop by Leo X in 1518, have learned the Sarum liturgy?

Again, we don't know, but these are serious historical possibilities. And by entertaining these possibilities, we are persuaded to abandon any facile stereotype of African primitivism. The court of Kongo might well have used a ritually complex medieval ceremonial that would make even today's Latin Mass parishes look bare and austere by comparison.

Does a Congolese liturgy really have to mean the modern Zairean Use? Or can it also mean the medieval Sarum Use as well? Perhaps all our focus on developing a new liturgy has distracted our attention from something far older and roots that run much deeper: a priceless liturgical heirloom still waiting to be discovered in a Congolese archive.

10

DID THE REFORMED LITURGICAL RITES CAUSE A BOOM IN MISSIONARY LANDS?

PETER KWASNIEWSKI

I ONCE RECEIVED THE FOLLOW-ing letter:

In my many discussions with fellow Catholics about the subject of the 20th century liturgical reforms, the objection often comes up that they directly coincide with the incredible explosion of Catholic faith in many parts of Africa and Asia.

I generally respond by saying that just because the totality of reforms may have had such positive impacts doesn't justify any particular one of them, and a dispensation could have been allowed to use some vernacular in the Mass in mission territories without the enormous overhaul that was done. However, I'm not sure this is a massively convincing response and wondered if you had ever given the idea some thought? It seems like a gap in pro-Traditonal Liturgy discourse to me. It seems that for the legitimate points to be made about reverence, attendance, understanding, and so on deteriorating after the promulgation of the 1969/1970 Missal, one also has to take into account the positive fruits of the post-Conciliar era.

My response was as follows.

African missions were experiencing consider-
able growth throughout the twentieth century,
including (as I'm sure you know) the missions
of the Holy Ghost Fathers under the guidance
of Archbishop Lefebvre. There is every reason to
believe that this upward trajectory would have
continued, quite possibly even stronger, had tradition not been derailed. There was no proof
that the traditional Roman rite was incapable of
being introduced and cultivated among natives
of many lands, together with a reserved and sen-
sible approach to inculturation, and some use of
the vernacular, especially for readings and music.

On a darker note, the loosening up of doctrine and worship after the Council has allowed
abuses to flourish in missionary lands, since a
patient and persistent will to curtail and correct
them was no longer operative: the mingling of
pagan and Christian rituals and beliefs, polygamy,
clerical concubinage, and so forth.

The growth witnessed in recent decades can
be accounted for demographically without the
need to invoke Vatican II or the reformed liturgy as a primary cause. This would seem to
be a classic case where the fallacy *post hoc ergo
propter hoc* might be operative — a fallacy that
has often been thrown in the faces of tradi-
tionalists when they argue that Vatican II and/

or the liturgical reform caused, or prompted, a massive decline in religious practice, at least in the Western nations. The latter claim, however, is at this point beyond dispute, whereas the claim that Vatican II and its reforms prompted the growth of churches in other parts of the world is by no means easy to argue. (Indeed, whether any good can be attributed to this Council has been and continues to be the subject of intense conversation.[1])

Catholicism in Asia was generally experiencing steady growth in the twentieth century with traditional modes of worship intact. A case in point: in China, the persecuted underground Church remained strong with the traditional Latin Mass until the late 1980s, when the Novus Ordo was first introduced with the collusion of the Communist Party.[2] The situation in China today certainly cannot be said to be superior to what is was before.[3] The Vietnamese were just as devout and single-minded in their Catholicism under tradition as under novelty, and today many who have rediscovered the TLM love it.

---

[1] See Kwasniewski, ed., *After Sixty Years,* for a broad spectrum of opinions by major Catholic writers.

[2] See "The Liturgical 'Reform' in China," *Rorate Caeli,* July 7, 2009.

[3] See Anthony E. Clark, "The Catholic Church in China: Historical Context and the Current Situation," *Catholic World Report,* March 9, 2018.

As the book *The Case for Liturgical Restoration* argues,[4] the Far Eastern mentality, broadly
speaking, is well-suited to the contemplative
ceremoniality and symbolism of the TLM (one
need only think of the famous Japanese tea
ceremony). Put differently, the novel aspects
of the Novus Ordo that some modern people
find appealing are the same aspects they will
find—albeit usually more successfully—in Protestant Evangelicals and Pentecostals. It is therefore hardly surprising that Third World countries
have experienced an explosion in conversions
to (and, tragically, Catholic defections to) such
Protestant sects. There are, needless to say, many
other factors as well, such as the clergy's drift
away from preaching the Word of God and
fostering sound popular devotions, into align-
ment with socialist political programs. For those
who are seeking God, for those who want to
be saved by Christ, this will be a major turn-off.

It is true that a concession for *some* use of
the vernacular was sought by *some* missionaries
(although we may note that a large number of
bishops at Vatican II spoke up *against* vernacu-
larization),[5] and there is no particular reason to

---

[4] Joseph Shaw, ed., *The Case for Liturgical Restoration:* Una
Voce *Studies on the Traditional Latin Mass* (Brooklyn, NY:
Angelico Press, 2019), esp. chs. 25, 31, and 32.

[5] See my trio of articles at *New Liturgical Movement:* "The

think that this concession is necessarily a bad idea. However, there is much in the Catholic liturgy that remains constant from day to day; *that* content should certainly remain in Latin.[6]

In my book *Reclaiming Our Roman Catholic Birthright*, I say the following (p. 12, n. 3), which I think is relevant to the topic at hand:

> That there have been a few saints after and under the Novus Ordo does not prove that it is equal in its sanctifying power to the traditional Latin Mass, just as the fact that some demons can be expelled by the new rite of exorcism does not contradict the general agreement of exorcists that the traditional Latin rite of exorcism is far more effective. At most, such things prove that God will not be thwarted by churchmen or their reforms. As theologians teach, God is not bound to His ordinances: He can sanctify souls outside of the use of sacraments, even though we are duty-bound to use the sacraments He has given us. Analogously, He can sanctify a loving soul through a liturgy deficient in tradition, reverence, beauty, and other qualities that ought to belong

---

Council Fathers in Support of Latin: Correcting a Narrative Bias," September 13, 2017; "What They Requested, What They Expected, and What Happened: Council Fathers on the Latin Roman Canon," August 8, 2022; "The Lie That Was Told to Over 2,000 Council Fathers at Vatican II," May 27, 2024.
[6] For a full defense of this claim, see my book *Turned Around: Replying to Common Objections Against the Traditional Latin Mass* (Gastonia, NC: TAN Books, 2024), 167–90, as well as the following chapter.

to it by natural and divine law, although in the normal course souls ought to avail themselves of these powerful aids to sanctity.

One might say something similar about "good fruits" after the liturgical reform. Are they precisely *because* of that reform, or are they rather *in spite of* it? God wills the salvation of mankind, so He will make use of whatever instrument the Church provides: a sharp knife or a blunt knife. The sharp knife will cut better, but the blunt knife will still serve in many cases. Yet it would be far better to have kept the sharp one, or to get it back as soon as possible.

Cordially in Christ,
Dr. Kwasniewski

11
HOW THE TRADITIONAL LITURGY CONTRIBUTES TO RACIAL AND ETHNIC INTEGRATION

PETER KWASNIEWSKI

THE RACIAL UNREST THAT flares up from time to time in the United States rightly prompts an examination of conscience: Are we complicit in the "structures of sin" that contribute to strained or abusive race relations? But one wonders if the soul-searching in Catholic circles is sufficiently deep, as opposed to skating on the surface of slogans.[1]

An observation I recently read—"since the United States was never a Catholic country, it has historically lacked the full means that Catholic nations had to unite the different races"—made me think about the liturgical resources for unity that the Church has historically possessed, and how her postconciliar rulers have squandered those resources thanks to a

---

[1] See Kevin Wells, "George Floyd and How the Church Abandoned the Inner Cities," *OnePeterFive*, June 5, 2020.

misguided movement of modernization, lowest-common-denominator localization, and narrowly-construed inculturation.

The old Latin liturgy united nations, clans, tribes, races. Everyone had (more or less) the same liturgy. It was in a high style, said in a language no longer anyone's vernacular, and therefore not the possession of any nation or party; it was celebrated "just so," in a way that was distinctively its own, because it came from so many centuries and influences. In an article for the *Southern Nebraska Register*, Fr. Justin Wylie wrote:

> Only a language owned by no one in particular belongs to everyone universally. Truly, Latin has rendered our Faith Catholic (which is to say, universal) in time and space. Babel's curse of linguistic segmentation was remedied by the Pentecost miracle of a Church that evangelizes all nations in a single tongue, with parity of understanding. The pagans of ancient Greece and Rome, Europe's barbarian tribes, and the New World's disparate peoples were evangelized by the common denominator of our Latin liturgy.

Even into modern times, one could see very diverse congregations gathered in the same church for the same Latin Mass, engaging with it in various ways depending on their needs and abilities: servants and their employers; rich and poor; "blue-collar" and "white-collar" workers;

the educated and the illiterate; devout daily Mass-goers and stubbornly dutiful Sunday regulars. Even if parishes were often set up along ethnic lines, there was still, beyond this, a strong sense of belonging to the one Catholic Church, the great equalizer and leveler.

Historian Henry Sire makes some mordant comments about the sociological results of the reform of the sixties:

> By cutting off the life of the Church from a timeless tradition, the Modernists have immersed it in a contemporary social setting. The foible is especially noticeable in Germany, where the radicalism of the reformers has produced a parish Mass of comically bourgeois style; but that is the tone of the modern liturgy in all the Western countries. In an ordinary Mass today the sense one has is not the offering of an eternal sacrifice but a lecture conducted by the priest and two or three women of the public-librarian class, to whom the readings and other duties of the church are allocated. The verbosity and preachiness of the liturgy is itself a middle-class characteristic with which many ordinary parishioners feel little rapport; and the alienation of working-class worshippers, in a way that was never true of the old Mass in poor parishes, has become a peculiar feature of the liturgical reform.[2]

---

[2] H. J. A. Sire, *Phoenix from the Ashes: The Making, Unmaking, and Restoration of Catholic Tradition* (Kettering, OH: Angelico Press, 2015), 264.

Sire's critique was empirically verified by the research of Anthony Archer in his 1984 study *The Two Catholic Churches*. As Joseph Shaw summarizes:

> Archer's critique of the changes after Vatican II is based on the fact that the aspects of the Church which were most appealing to the working class were swept away, and what was brought in was appealing only to the educated and leisured middle class. Out went the Latin Mass in which everyone could engage at their own level; in came an English Mass where your engagement is supposed to be strictly controlled: exactly what the banal phrases mean, what responses to make, when to be friendly to your neighbour, etc. Out went popular devotions, in came cliquey little groups at house-Masses, charismatic gatherings, or parish councils. Out went the Church as a sign of contradiction, an eccentric, exotic refuge from society, where truth and authority were alone to be found; in came a Church in which the bishops talked as equals to Anglican bishops, and attended state functions. Out went the spirituality of perseverence in adversity; in came a way of "finding Jesus" to escape from middle class problems such as loneliness and depression—or just hypochondria. The inspiration for the changes, after all, did not come from any attempt to find out what the bulk of Catholics wanted: it came from theologians, who wanted the respect of their Protestant colleagues.[3]

---

[3] See Joseph Shaw, "A Sociologist on the Latin Mass," *LMS Chairman*, June 26, 2013, and "The Old Mass and the

To summarize: the liturgical reform homogenized and narrowed the reach of Catholic liturgy, in particular cutting off all those people (and they are, and will always be, very numerous) to whom immediate verbal and rational comprehension of people-directed vernacular discourse with obligatory responses is not an appealing mode of engagement, or worse, is an impediment to prayerful engagement.

The imposition of the vernacular and the lack of ritual and rubrical discipline has separated us into little enclaves. You end up with Masses for white upper-middle-class golfers, Mass with African-American Gospel music, Mass for Hispanics, Mass for Vietnamese, etc. etc. How can the Church "unite the different races" if she can't even unite us in a single recognizably Catholic worship?

Thus the aforementioned Fr. Wylie, who grew up in South Africa, notes with sadness:

> Apartheid did less to divide Catholics of many races in South Africa than the introduction of the vernacular in the liturgy, for whereas before, these worshipped together easily in Latin, since its loss, they now find themselves deeply divided at diocesan celebrations.

My experience with TLM communities around the world has been dramatically different from

---

Workers," *LMS Chairman*, July 3, 2013. The passage quoted is from the second of these articles.

this widespread liturgical segregation. Almost everywhere I go, but especially in urban parishes, I see different races and ethnicities side by side in the pews: Asians, African-Americans, Africans, whites of all European backgrounds.[4] The commonness of the worship and its deep reverence unite us all. The traditional Latin liturgy chanted by the minister and choir in the church is one and common to all, binding us together as a fixed, stable, reliable, external "gold standard." It is the center of gravity that draws us all towards Christ—and therefore towards each other. Prayer happens within and between the ancient Latin chanted aloud, the modern vernacular quietly available, and the prayer of the worshiper's heart, which transcends all linguistic differences.

When I say "the vernacular quietly available," I mean translations contained in a hand missal or a leaflet as an aid to understanding, a ladder to climb up, "training wheels" for the bicycle, as indeed they were for me for many years. Trads are not snobs about this; we are very pragmatic. Whatever helps, helps. Vernacular translations hold out a welcoming hand to those who are not familiar with the liturgical

---

[4] I am not saying, of course, that no Novus Ordo communities are possessed of such diversity, nor that no TLM communities could ever be described as single-demographic. Rather, I am pointing to some broader trends that I have seen myself and heard from others, in both the NOM and TLM worlds.

texts, and help them to ponder their meaning. At the same time, such translations never have to be "official translations," the diction and style of which are endlessly fought over in committees, with results no one is ever really pleased with; the old-rite missal translations fortunately do not have to bear such weight. The Latin text bears *all* the ritual and theological weight, while the vernacular is free to be read in its several variations—or to be ignored. From this point of view, the TLM community offers far more realistic possibilities for multilingual congregations, since its more compact missal-cum-lectionary has already been conveniently translated into many major languages. In an urban congregation, it is not uncommon to find hand missals in half a dozen different languages being used at the same liturgy: truly *the same* liturgy.

In his masterpiece *Democracy in America*, published between 1835 and 1840, Alexis de Tocqueville describes a Catholic Church that seems almost no longer to exist:

> On doctrinal points the Catholic faith places all human capacities upon the same level; it subjects the wise and ignorant, the man of genius and the vulgar crowd, to the details of the same creed; it imposes the same observances upon the rich and the needy, it inflicts the same austerities upon the strong and the weak; it listens to no compromise with mortal

man, but, reducing all the human race to the same standard, it confounds all the distinctions of society at the foot of the same altar, even as they are confounded in the sight of God. If Catholicism predisposes the faithful to obedience, it certainly does not prepare them for inequality; but the contrary may be said of Protestantism, which generally tends to make men independent more than to render them equal. Catholicism is like an absolute monarchy; if the sovereign be removed, all the other classes of society are more equal than in republics.[5]

Churchmen after the Council foolishly abandoned this remarkable power of a single Creed, acknowledged and taught as such; a single observance with real asceticism; and, above all, a common body of Latin liturgy to draw together people of different races, ethnicities, languages, classes, backgrounds, and vocations. We may truly say that the practice of the traditional liturgy has been, and is capable of becoming once again, the Catholic Church's "secret weapon" for unity among the faithful of the far-flung and demographically highly diverse Latin rite. The Collect of Easter Tuesday beautifully captures this aspiration, reflected in the very externals of the traditional Roman rite:

---

[5] Alexis de Tocqueville, *Democracy in America,* trans. Henry Reeve, rev. Francis Bowen (Cambridge: Sever and Francis, 1863), vol. 1, pp. 384–85.

> O God, Who dost make all nations, how diverse
> soever they be, to become one family in giving
> praise to thy Name, grant unto all those who
> are born again in the fountain of baptism to live
> ever in oneness of faith and godliness of works.

The world needs genuine signs and sources of unity more than ever, not farces like white people claiming to "renounce their whiteness" (or, for that matter, Catholics renouncing their own great tradition). We need to find our unity and healing not in social justice campaigns or police reforms, whatever value those may have in their way, but in the grace and truth of the *one* Savior of mankind and His *one* Church, vividly symbolized, in the Roman patriarchate, by a common Latin liturgical inheritance embodied in the *usus antiquior.*

BIBLIOGRAPHY

Achebe, Chinua. *Things Fall Apart*. New York: Anchor Books, 1994.

Agbo, Benedict Nwabugwu. "Inculturation of Liturgical Music in the Roman Catholic Church of Igbo Land: A Compositional Study." *Journal of Global Catholicism*, vol. 1, no. 2 (2017): 6–27.

Alimnonu, O.A. "Review of Austin Echema, *Corporate Personality in Traditional Igbo Society and the Sacrament of Reconciliation*." *Bulletin of Ecumenical Theology*, vol. 8, no. 2 (1996): 66–69.

Anonymous ["AP"]. "The Liturgical 'Reform' in China." *Rorate Caeli*, July 7, 2009.

Anyanwu, Cajetan. "Reshaping the Theology and Praxis of Inculturation through Interreligious Dialogue Between the Catholic Church and African Traditional Religion in Igboland, Nigeria." Doctoral Thesis, Duquesne University, 2019.

Auclair, Marcelle. *Teresa of Avila*. New York: Doubleday Image, 1959.

Baldwin, Marshall W. *The Mediaeval Church*. New York: Cornell University Press, 1953.

Benedict, Ruth. "The Growth of Culture." In H.L. Shapiro, ed., *Man, Culture, and Society*, 182–95. New York: Oxford University Press, 1956.

Bowie, Fiona. "The Inculturation Debate in Africa." *Studies in World Christianity*, vol. 5, no. 1 (2011): 67–92.

Carroll, Warren H. *The Building of Christendom*. Front Royal, VA: Christendom College Press, 1987.

Cavadini, John, Mary Healy, and Thomas Weinandy. "The Way Forward from the Theological Concerns with the TLM Movement." *Church Life Journal*, November 23, 2022.

Chase, Nathan P. "A History and Analysis of the *Missel Romain pour les Dioceses du Zaire*." *Obsculta* vol. 6, no. 1 (2013): 28–36.

Chiorazzi, Anthony. "The Spirituality of Africa." *The Harvard Gazette*, October 6, 2015.

Clark, Anthony E. "The Catholic Church in China: Historical Context and the Current Situation." *Catholic World Report, March 9, 2018.*

Coleman, Willi. *"Elizabeth Taylor Greenfield." Blackpast,* March 27, 2007. www.blackpast.org/african-american-history/greenfield-elizabeth-taylor-1819-1876/.

Copeland, M. Shawn, ed. *Uncommon Faithfulness: The Black Catholic Experience.* Maryknoll, NY: Orbis Books, 2009.

Cormack, Margaret, ed. *Saints and Their Cults in the Atlantic World.* Columbia, SC: University of South Carolina Press, 2007.

Cressler, Matthew J. *"African Catholics and Slave Rebellion in Early American History."* Religion in American History, January 31, 2014.

D'Emilio, Frances. "Joyous Congolese Dances, Songs Enliven St. Peter's Basilica." *Voice of America,* English news, December 1, 2019, story by Associated Press.

Dewulf, Jeroen. *From the Kingdom of Kongo to the Congo Square: Kongo Dances and the Origins of the Mardi Gras Indians.* Lafayette: University of Louisiana at Lafayette Press, 2017.

Donnelly, Eleanor C. *A Memoir of Father Felix Joseph Barbelin, SJ.* New York: Christian Press Association Publishing Company, 1886.

Douthat, Ross. "How Catholics Became Prisoners of Vatican II" and "How Vatican II Failed Catholics—and Catholicism. In Kwasniewski, *Sixty Years After: Catholic Writers Assess the Legacy of Vatican II,* 63–73.

Doyle, Dennis M. "The Concept of Inculturation in Roman Catholicism: A Theological Consideration." Religious Studies Faculty Publications, 2012. https://ecommons.udayton.edu/rel_fac_pub/102.

Duchesne, Louis. *Christian Worship: Its Origin and Evolution.* London: Society for Promoting Christian Knowledge, 1904.

Ekwunife, A.N.O. "African Traditional Values and Formation in Catholic Seminaries of Nigeria." *Bulletin of Ecumenical Theology,* vol. 8, no. 2 (1996): 49–65.

Griffin, Martin IJ., ed. "Chateaubriand in Philadelphia 1791—Composes a Hymn for the Colored Catholics." *The American Catholic Historical Researches for 1899,* 151. Philadelphia:

Martin IJ. Griffin, 1899. May be found at Google Books by searching "hail happy queen chateaubriand."

Griffin, Martin I. J. History of "Old St. Joseph's" Philadelphia. Philadelphia: I.C.B.U. Journal Print, 1882.

Grimes, Robert R. How Shall We Sing in a Foreign Land? Notre Dame, IN: University of Notre Dame Press, 1996.

Grossman, Cathy Lynn. "More Catholics, fewer receiving sacraments: A new report maps a changing church." Religion News Service, June 1, 2015.

Hayden, Augustine. Ireland's Loyalty to the Mass. Manchester, NH: Sophia Institute Press, 2023.

Hodge, Brendan. "Demography reigns down in Africa." The Pillar, December 29, 2021.

Inyanwachi, Edward. "A Content Analysis of Church Documents Relative to the Role of Catholic Schools and Universities in Nigeria in the Process of Inculturation." Doctoral Thesis, University of San Francisco, 2007.

John Paul II. Post-Synodal Apostolic Exhortation Ecclesia in Africa. September 14, 1995.

Jones, Kenneth C. Index of Leading Catholic Indicators: The Church since Vatican II. Fort Collins, CO: Roman Catholic Books, 2003.

Jungmann, Josef A. The Mass of the Roman Rite: Its Origins and Development. Westminster, MD: Christian Classics, 1986.

Kantor, Marvin. "A Brief Account of Saints Cyril and Methodius and the Baptism of the Moravian and Bohemian Lands." In Norman E. Thomas, ed., Classic Texts in Mission and World Christianity. New York: Orbis Books, 1995.

Kanu, Ikechukwu Anthony. "Inculturation and the Christian Faith in Africa." International Journal of Humanities and Social Science, vol. 2, no. 17 (2012): 236–44.

Kwasniewski, Peter. "The Council Fathers in Support of Latin: Correcting a Narrative Bias." New Liturgical Movement, September 13, 2017.

——. "The Lie That Was Told to Over 2,000 Council Fathers at Vatican II." New Liturgical Movement, May 27, 2024.

——. Reclaiming Our Roman Catholic Birthright: The Genius and Timeliness of the Traditional Latin Mass. Brooklyn, NY: Angelico Press, 2020.

——. *Sixty Years After: Catholic Writers Assess the Legacy of Vatican II*. Brooklyn, NY: Angelico Press, 2022.

——. *Turned Around: Replying to Common Objections Against the Traditional Latin Mass*. Gastonia, NC: TAN Books, 2024.

——. "What They Requested, What They Expected, and What Happened: Council Fathers on the Latin Roman Canon." New Liturgical Movement, August 8, 2022

Lewis, C.S. *Mere Christianity*. New York: Macmillan Publishing Company, 1952.

Mares, Courtney. "Pope Francis celebrates Mass in the Congolese rite: 'Peace begins with us.'" *Catholic News Agency*, July 3, 2022.

Martin, György. "Dance Types in Ethiopia." *Journal of the International Folk Music Council*, vol. 19 (1967): 23–27.

McDaniel, Doris Anna. "Analysis of the Missa Luba," Master's Thesis, University of Rochester, 1973.

Millot, René Pierre. *Missions in the World Today*. New York: Hawthorn Books, 1961.

Nche, George C., Lawrence N. Okwuosa, and Theresa C. Nwaoga. "Revisiting the Concept of Inculturation in a Modern Africa: A Reflection on Salient Issues." *HTS Teologiese Studies/Theological Studies*, vol. 72, no. 1 (2016).

Niebuhr, H. Richard. *Christ and Culture*. New York: Harper & Row, 1951.

Njoku, Francis O.C. "Some Indigenous Models in African Theology and an Ethic of Inculturation." *Bulletin of Ecumenical Theology*, vol. 8, no. 2 (1996): 4–32.

Nouveau, Christophe. *The Role of the Traditional Latin Mass in the Evangelisation of the Catholic Church in Uganda (1879–1969)*. N.p.: Blessed Hope Publishing, 2022.

Okwu, A.S.O. "Life, Death, Reincarnation, and Traditional Healing in Africa." *Issue: A Journal of Opinion*, vol. 9, no. 3 (1979): 19–24.

Onyewuenyi, Innocent C. "A Philosophical Reappraisal of African Belief in Reincarnation." *Présence Africaine*, new series, vol. 123 (1982): 63–78. The same article was published in vol. 22 of the *International Philosophical Quarterly*.

Paul VI. "Address to the Members of the Catholic Church in Uganda." August 1, 1969.

Perczel, Csilla Fabo. "Art and Liturgy: Abyssinian Processional Crosses." *Northeast African Studies*, vol. 5, no. 1 (1983): 19–28.

Perry, Joseph. "Black Catholic Worship: Some Reflections." *American Catholic Press.* www.americancatholicpress.org/Bishop_%20Perry_Black_Catholic_Worship.html.

Pew Research Center. "Overview: Pentecostalism in Africa." October 5, 2006. www.pewresearch.org/religion/2006/10/05/overview-pentecostalism-in-africa/.

Pius X. Instruction on Sacred Music *Tra Le Sollecitudini.* November 22, 1903.

Pius XII. Encyclical Letter *Evangelii Praecones.* June 2, 1951.

Presmanes, Jorge. "Inculturation as Evangelization: The Dialogue of Faith and Culture in the Work of Marcello Azevedo." *U.S. Catholic Historian*, vol. 30, no. 1 (2012): 59–76.

Reese, Thomas. "Global Catholic population up, number of priests down since 1980." *National Catholic Reporter*, June 1, 2015.

Rukiyanto, Bernardus A. "Interculturation as Threefold Dialogue: Learning Experience from the Church in Asia." *UTP Journals*, vol. 30, no. 2 (2007): 165–73.

Salamone, Frank A., and Michael C. Mbabuike. "The Plight of the Indigenous Catholic Priest in Africa: An Igbo Example." *Africa*, vol. 49, no. 2 (1994): 210–24.

Salvucci, Claudio. "The Amazon Synod, and the Liberal Enemies of Inculturation." October 10, 2019, https://hoquessing.com/the-amazon-synod-and-the-liberal-enemies-of-inculturation/.

———. "Images of the Catholic Congo." *Liturgical Arts Journal*, November 23, 2017.

———. *The Roman Rite in the Algonquian and Iroquoian Missions from the Colonial Period to the Second Vatican Council.* Merchantville, NJ: Evolution Publishing, 2008.

Schuster, Ildefonso. *The Sacramentary.* Volume 1. London: Burns, Oates & Washbourne, 1924.

Second Vatican Ecumenical Council. Constitution on the Sacred Liturgy *Sacrosanctum Concilium.* December 4, 1963.

Shaw, Joseph, ed. *The Case for Liturgical Restoration: Una Voce Studies on the Traditional Latin Mass.* Brooklyn, NY: Angelico Press, 2019.

Shaw, Joseph. "The Old Mass and the Workers." *LMS Chairman*, July 3, 2013.

———. "A Sociologist on the Latin Mass." *LMS Chairman*, June 26, 2013.

Sire, H.J.A. *Phoenix from the Ashes: The Making, Unmaking, and Restoration of Catholic Tradition*. Kettering, OH: Angelico Press, 2015.

Smith, Janet E. "Unity, Charismatic Masses, and Africa." In Peter A. Kwasniewski, ed., *Illusions of Reform: Responses to Cavadini, Healy, and Weinandy in Defense of the Traditional Mass and the Faithful Who Attend It*, 41–45. Lincoln, NE: Os Justi Press, 2023.

Stefaniszyn, B. "African Reincarnation Re-examined." *African Studies*, vol. 13, nos. 3–4 (1954): 131–46.

Thornton, John. "The Development of an African Catholic Church in the Kingdom of Kongo, 1491–1750." *The Journal of African History*, vol. 25, no. 2 (1984): 147–67.

Tocqueville, Alexis de. *Democracy in America*, trans. Henry Reeve, rev. Francis Bowen. Cambridge: Sever and Francis, 1863.

Tourigny, Yves. *So Abundant a Harvest: The Catholic Church in Uganda 1879–1979*. London: Darton, Longman and Todd, 1979.

Twomey, D. Vincent. *The End of Irish Catholicism?* Dublin: Veritas Publications, 2003.

"Vatican: Islam Surpasses Roman Catholicism as World's Largest Religion." *Associated Press*, March 30, 2008. www.foxnews.com/story/vatican-islam-surpasses-roman-catholicism-as-worlds-largest-religion.

Wells, Kevin. "George Floyd and How the Church Abandoned the Inner Cities." *OnePeterFive, June 5, 2020.*

Wielzen, Duncan. "Popular Religiosity and Roman Liturgy: Toward a Contemporary Theology of Liturgical Inculturation in the Caribbean." Doctoral Thesis, Katholieke Universiteit Leuven, 2009.

Woods, Thomas E. *How the Catholic Church Built Western Civilization*. Washington, DC: Regnery Publishing, 2005.

www.ingramcontent.com/pod-product-compliance
Lightning Source LLC
Chambersburg PA
CBHW060236030426
42335CB00014B/1482